Beantown Sports Trivia

Matthew Silverman

Blue River Press
Indianapolis, IN

Cover designed by Phil Velikan
Editorial assistance provided by Dorothy Chambers
Packaged by Wish Publishing

Printed in the United States of America
10 9 8 7 6 5 4 3 2 1

Published by Blue River Press
Distributed by Cardinal Publishers Group
Tom Doherty Company, Inc.
www.cardinalpub.com

Table of Contents

THE PATRIOTS

THE RED SOX

Introduction

Having lived in both New England and New York, I will say that of the two, New England is a bit more rabid when it comes to sports. New York knows its sports, but it tends to be so fragmented through nine professional teams and does not really have a major college presence. New England, on the other hand, is more like one long, six-state neighborhood where most everybody is watching the same game on TV, celebrating the same victory, or licking the same wound. A community of the fanatical.

And Boston not only has the greatest concentration of colleges in the country, it also has the greatest concentration of different college sports. It might have gotten lighter on the college football in recent years, but Massachusetts can always lay claim to the invention of basketball, and no regular-season college tournament cooks it up like the annual Beanpot, which began with hockey six decades ago and has spilled onto many other plates in many different sports, for men and women.

Corralling the college section was the hardest part of this book, but extreme effort was made to include many different schools, with questions that might be answered by alumni and educated guessers alike. The four original Beanpot schools—Boston College, Boston University, Harvard and Northeastern—have their own sections, plus a couple of "bridge" sections have been added to highlight certain rivalries.

The pro teams are broken up a little differently, and include other short question areas to keep you on your toes. The main sections are broken into three parts:

1. The majority of questions will be under a general heading about recent events, seasons or players.
2. "Your Father's Team (Sox, Pats, Bruins, Celtics)"— generally questions before 1985.
3. "Your Grandfather's Team"—generally questions from 1967 or earlier. (Because the Red Sox have been around the longest, they earned a special category for great-grandfathers.)

Keeping Score

Questions are a combination of short answer, multiple choice, and true and false. For those keeping score, the initial parts of each section will be worth one point each. The father, grandfather, and in the case of the Red Sox, great-grandfather questions are worth two points. It can even be called "Going for Two." Because there is enough studying and formulas to keep straight in school, we're keeping it easy by making every college question worth one point. But there are grades for those who crave final scores.

Colleges, Bruins and Celtics can be graded as such:

130 or better: Man the Duck Boats for the parade!

100-129: Got to Game 7 but took it on the chin

70-99: Playoff caliber

40-69: There's always next year

0-39: Rebuilding Mode

The Red Sox have the most questions—because they're the Sox, that's why!—so the top grade for the Olde Towne Team is anything over 230, with a perfect score of 247. The Patriots have a top score of 200 out of a possible 216. (If you're so fond of math, figure out your percentage and run that against the above chart.) And because we care, consider the seven Boxing and Golf questions to be extra credit—one point each.

And if you got an absolutely perfect score of 924 out of 924, maybe you should go back and take the SATs again.

The Bruins

Bruins Basics

1. Marc Savard's two goals and two assists against the Canadiens in Game 2 of the first round of the 2009 playoffs marked the first time a Bruin had recorded four points in a postseason game since which Bruin did it in 1996?

   A. Ray Bourque

   B. Ted Donato

   C. Cam Neely

   D. Adam Oates

2. When was the last year the Bruins raised the Stanley Cup before 2011?

   A. 1968

   B. 1970

   C. 1972

   D. 1974

3. Who has sung the national anthem at Bruins games for more than 30 seasons?

4. List the four postseason opponents defeated by the Bruins en route to the 2010-11 Stanley Cup.

5. In 2003-04, the last year that ties were permitted in the NHL, the Bruins had how many "kiss your sister" evenings during the regular season?

A. 5

B. 10

C. 15

D. 20

6. How many consecutive years did the Bruins reach the playoffs starting in 1966-67?

A. 20

B. 25

C. 30

D. 35

7. What was the longstanding name of the Bruins' division before it simply became known as the Northeast Division?

8. During the 19 years of the Adams Division's existence (1974-1993), the Bruins won more division titles than any other team. How many did they win?

9. What college did Stanley Cup champion goalie Tim Thomas attend before turning pro?

A. Clarkson University

B. McGill University

C. University of North Dakota

D. University of Vermont

10. Which relocated NHL franchise originally selected Tim Thomas in the 1994 draft?

A. Atlanta Thrashers

B. Hartford Whalers

C. Minnesota North Stars

D. Quebec Nordiques

11. Coach Claude Julien took over the Bruins in which season?

A. 2002-03

B. 2005-06

C. 2007-08

D. 2009-10

12. True or false? The Bruins and Canadiens have played more postseason series against each other than any pair of opponents in NHL history.

13. Which team has won more playoff series against each other: the Canadiens or Bruins?

14. In the first round of the 2011 playoffs, the Bruins rallied from two games to none for the first time in franchise history. How many times had the Bruins lost after facing this deficit before?

A. 7

B. 17

C. 27

D. 37

15. What is the longest stretch the Bruins have gone without a postseason appearance?

    A. 8 years

    B. 12 years

    C. 16 years

    D. 20 years

16. Especially vexing in the Montreal-Boston hockey rivalry is that the Canadiens had beaten the Bruins in the deciding game four times before Boston finally took a Game 7 from Montreal. What year did that finally happen?

    A. 1951

    B. 1971

    C. 1991

    D. 2011

17. Ray Bourque never won a Stanley Cup in 21 seasons with the Bruins. What team did he go to and win the Cup in his 22nd and final season?

    A. Colorado Avalanche

    B. Detroit Red Wings

    C. Montreal Canadiens

    D. Tampa Bay Lightning

18. Who scored two overtime goals against the Canadiens in the 2011 playoffs, including the game winner in Game 7 in Boston?

    A. Zdeno Chara

    B. Andrew Ference

    C. Nathan Horton

    D. Michael Ryder

19. The Bruins opened the 2010-11 season winning two games in Prague. Who was Boston's unlucky NHL Premiere opponent in the Czech Republic?

A. Anaheim Ducks

B. Montreal Canadiens

C. New Jersey Devils

D. Phoenix Coyotes

20. Which team did the Bruins beat in the Winter Classic at Fenway Park on January 1, 2010?

A. Montreal Canadiens

B. Philadelphia Flyers

C. Pittsburgh Penguins

D. Washington Capitals

21. Who was the only Bruin in history to play on three Stanley Cup champion teams?

A. Johnny Bucyk

B. Dit Clapper

C. Milt Schmidt

D. Eddie Shore

22. Through 2011, who was the only Bruin in history to be employed by the team for four Stanley Cup championships?

A. Johnny Bucyk

B. Dit Clapper

C. Milt Schmidt

D. Eddie Shore

23. How many feet shorter was the Boston Garden ice surface than the standard NHL hockey rink?

A. 3 feet

B. 6 feet

C. 9 feet

D. 12 feet

24. A power failure at Boston Garden in 1988 resulted in Game 4 of the NHL finals being declared a tie. Which Boston opponent was left in the dark?

A. Calgary Flames

B. Detroit Red Wings

C. Edmonton Oilers

D. Montreal Canadiens

25. Which Bruins goalie was the last to play in every game of the season?

A. Frank Brimsek

B. Gerry Cheevers

C. Eddie Johnston

D. Tiny Thompson

26. What Bruin said he would retire if the Bruins won the 2010-11 Stanley Cup?

27. Which Bruins Hall of Famer and all-time top goal scorer claimed his third Stanley Cup while serving as the team's road services coordinator in 2010-11?

28. Through 2011, what are the only two single-digit numbers not retired by the Bruins?

29. Through 2011, which Bruin had appeared in the most All-Star Games?
    A. Ray Bourque
    B. Johnny Bucyk
    C. Gerry Cheevers
    D. Cam Neely

30. Stanley Cup-winning Bruins goalies Gerry Cheevers and Tim Thomas wore what uniform number?

31. Who gave up number 7 on a night the Bruins were honoring Phil Esposito so the number could be hauled to the rafters at Boston Garden?

32. Four Bruins have pulled off winning a Stanley Cup, earning a Hart Trophy, being inducted into the Hall of Fame, and having his number retired by the Bruins. Name this impressive Bruins quartet.

33. Who was the last Bruins coach before Claude Julien to last more than four years?

A. Gerry Cheevers

B. Mike Milbury

C. Terry O'Reilly

D. Harry Sinden

34. What former Bruins goaltending great became a Pittsburgh executive and drafted Mario Lemieux?

A. Gerry Cheevers

B. Gilles Gilbert

C. Eddie Johnston

D. Pete Peeters

35. Stanley Cup-winning Bruins general manager Peter Chiarelli played hockey at which "Beanpot" school?

A. Boston College

B. Boston University

C. Harvard

D. Northeastern

36. What 2011 Stanley Cup-winning Bruins executive ranks third all time in Bruins history in games played?

37. What former Stanley Cup-winning Bruin was tragically killed in the September 11, 2001 attacks on New York City?

38. November 2011 was the first month the Bruins didn't suffer a loss in regulation since January of what year?

    A. 1959

    B. 1969

    C. 1979

    D. 1989

39. What team did the Bruins beat in the 2011 conference finals to reach the Stanley Cup final for the first time since 1990?

40. Who was the coach of the Bruins in 1990, the last year before 2011 in which they reached the Stanley Cup finals?

    A. Butch Goring

    B. Mike Milbury

    C. Terry O'Reilly

    D. Brent Sutter

41. Who was the first—and through 2011, the only—Bruins goalie to amass 40 wins during the regular season?

    A. Gerry Cheevers

    B. Pete Peeters

    C. Tim Thomas

    D. Tiny Thompson

42. Which goalie has played the most playoff games in Bruins history?

A. Frank Brimsek

B. Gerry Cheevers

C. Eddie Johnston

D. Tim Thomas

43. Two goalies, who were on the roster at the same time, share the club record for most assists by a Bruins netminder in a season, with four. Which was the most offensive goalie combo?

A. Gerry Cheevers, Eddie Johnston

B. Andy Moog, Rejean Lemelin

C. Tim Thomas, Tuukka Rask

D. Rogie Vachon, Jim Craig

44. On December 8, 1987, the Bruins were victimized by the first goal off the stick of a goalie in NHL history. Who scored it?

A. Martin Brodeur

B. Ron Hextall

C. Chris Osgood

D. Billy Smith

45. True or false? The Bruins have not won a Presidents' Trophy since it was first handed out in 1986 for the best regular-season record in the NHL.

46. Which team did the Bruins play in the final game at Boston Garden in 1995?

A. Montreal Canadiens

B. New Jersey Devils

C. New York Islanders

D. New York Rangers

47. Which team did the Bruins face in the first regular-season game at the Fleet Center (now known as TD Garden)?

A. Montreal Canadiens

B. New Jersey Devils

C. New York Islanders

D. New York Rangers

48. The Bruins were involved in 71 fights in 2011, the most altercations by a Stanley Cup winner since another year the Bruins reached the finals. What year was it?

A. 1970

B. 1972

C. 1988

D. 1990

49. Bruins captain Zdeno Chara is the tallest player in NHL history. At what height is the Slovak defenseman listed at?

50. True or false? Massachusetts has produced more American-born players than any state.

Answers on pages 38-42

Fight Night

1. Which Bruin took part in the first NHL fight in Winter Classic history?

    A. Gregory Campbell

    B. Zdeno Chara

    C. Milan Lucic

    D. Shawn Thornton

2. Which Canadien was suspended the rest of the 1955 season after knocking out a referee following an altercation at Boston Garden?

    A. Bernie "Boom Boom" Geoffrion

    B. Hal Laycoe

    C. Guy Lafleur

    D. Maurice "Rocket" Richard

3. Several Bruins climbed into the stands to fight fans at which arena on December 23, 1979?

    A. Boston Garden

    B. Madison Square Garden

    C. Nassau Coliseum

    D. Philadelphia Spectrum

4. Which Bruin hit a fan with the fan's shoe during Boston's fabled fight in the stands at Madison Square Garden on December 23, 1979?

    A. Peter McNab

    B. Mike Milbury

    C. Terry O'Reilly

    D. Brad Park

5. The most penalty-filled game of the 20th century was played on February 26, 1981, between the Bruins and which since-relocated team?

   A. Colorado Rockies

   B. Minnesota North Stars

   C. Quebec Nordiques

   D. Winnipeg Jets

6. The 1981 Bruins brawl set an NHL record with how many penalty minutes?

   A. 208

   B. 276

   C. 338

   D. 392

7. In the 1981 brawlfest at Boston Garden, how long did it take for the first fight to ensue?

   A. 7 seconds

   B. 27 seconds

   C. 47 seconds

   D. Before the opening faceoff

8. The 1981 brawlfest at Boston Garden saw how many players ejected in the first period?

   A. 4

   B. 8

   C. 12

   D. 16

Answers on pages 43-44

Your Father's Bruins

1. What pair of brothers played together with the 1982-84 Bruins?

2. When the Adams Division was formed in 1974, it had four NHL teams. Which now-defunct team was part of the division?

   A. California Golden Seals

   B. Cleveland Barons

   C. Kansas City Scouts

   D. Minnesota North Stars

3. For the 1979-80 season, the National Hockey League absorbed five World Hockey Association teams and expanded the playoffs to 16 teams from how many teams the year before?

   A. 6

   B. 8

   C. 10

   D. 12

4. What year did Ray Bourque win the Calder Memorial Trophy as the NHL's top rookie?

   A. 1978

   B. 1980

   C. 1982

   D. 1984

5. The Hall of Fame Montreal goalie who shattered many Boston dreams in the 1970s was actually Bruins property at one point. Who was this enemy goalie?

   A. Gary Cheevers

   B. Ken Dryden

   C. Emile Francis

   D. Glenn Hall

6. In Game 1 of the 1972 Stanley Cup finals, the Bruins blew a 5-1 lead over the Rangers only to win in the closing seconds on a goal by which Bruin?

   A. Ace Bailey

   B. Johnny Bucyk

   C. Phil Esposito

   D. Bobby Orr

7. The engraver spelled the team's name "BQSTQN BRUINS" on the 1972 Stanley Cup. What else was unique about the Bruins on that Cup?

   A. Bobby Orr's name was spelled "Bqbby Qrr."

   B. Captain Ed Westfall's name was left off.

   C. The names of every player had appeared on the Cup previously.

   D. The top of the Cup was dented during the celebration.

8. After the 1970-71 season the Bruins gave each of their 100-point scorers a golden puck. Name three of the four "golden" boys.

9. What Bruins great was lured from the Stanley Cup winners to the World Hockey Association in 1972 and became the highest-paid athlete in the world?

A. Gerry Cheevers

B. John McKenzie

C. Bobby Orr

D. Derek Sanderson

10. Who coached the Bruins to their last Stanley Cup before 2011?

A. Don Cherry

B. Bep Guidolin

C. Tom Johnson

D. Harry Sinden

11. This 1970s defenseman called Boston Garden "a dump" only to be traded to Boston in exchange for mega-popular Phil Esposito. Who was this ex-Ranger with his foot in his mouth?

12. Which team knocked off the Bruins and won the Stanley Cup in 1971, the year in between Bruins Cup triumphs?

A. Chicago Blackhawks

B. Montreal Canadiens

C. New York Rangers

D. Philadelphia Flyers

13. The 1970 Stanley Cup-champion Bruins team had the fewest number of players listed on any Cup in the post-expansion era. How many men were part of this "happy few"?

A. 16

B. 18

C. 20

D. 22

14. Which 1970 Bruin said the team would win "five or six" more Stanley Cups only to see himself taken in the expansion draft and wind up playing against the Bruins in the 1972 Stanley Cup finals?

A. Gary Doak

B. Don Marcotte

C. John McKenzie

D. Eddie Westphall

15. When Phil Esposito set the NHL goal-scoring mark in 1971, by how many goals did he break the record?

A. 1

B. 6

C. 12

D. 18

16. A crucial penalty late in the third period of Game 7 of the 1979 conference finals resulted in the game being tied. The Bruins lost in overtime. Who was the coach fired over it?

17. The Bruins had consecutive Calder Memorial Trophy winners for the top NHL rookie two years running in 1967 and 1968. Who were the award winners?

18. Bobby Orr was the first player to twice be named MVP of the playoffs. What is the name of this trophy he twice hoisted?

    A. Calder Cup

    B. Conn Smythe Trophy

    C. Lady Byng Memorial Trophy

    D. Vezina Trophy

19. What Bruin was the leading scorer and recorded the first goal of the legendary 1972 Summit Series between Team Canada and the U.S.S.R.?

20. Which two Bruins in 1970-71 became the first teammates to ever reach 50 goals in a season?

Answers on pages 44-46

The Bobby Orr Challenge

1. What jersey number did the Bruins retire for Bobby Orr?

2. Which of the following was significant about the signing of Bobby Orr's first contract with the Bruins in 1966?

   A. It was the first contract negotiated by an agent.

   B. Orr became the highest-paid player in NHL history.

   C. The contract was signed aboard a boat.

   D. All of the above.

3. One of the most famous hockey photographs is of Bobby Orr flying through the air after being tripped as he scored the overtime goal that won the 1970 Stanley Cup. What team did Orr's goal beat?

   A. Montreal Canadiens

   B. New York Rangers

   C. Philadelphia Flyers

   D. St. Louis Blues

4. True of false? Bobby Orr was the first defenseman to ever win a scoring title.

5. Name the two all-time legends who played after Bobby Orr and matched his feat of recording 100 assists in an NHL season.

6. Which all-time great defenseman broke Bobby Orr's career plus/minus mark of 597?

   A. Ray Bourque

   B. Brad Park

   C. Larry Robinson

   D. Serge Savard

7. After Bobby Orr's acrimonious split with the Bruins, which team did he join as a free agent?

   A. Chicago Blackhawks

   B. Minnesota North Stars

   C. New York Rangers

   D. Winnipeg Jets

8. Not only did the Hockey Hall of Fame waive the three-year wait period for Bobby Orr, but he was the youngest living player in history inducted into the Hockey Hall of Fame. How old was he when elected?

   A. 31

   B. 33

   C. 35

   D. 37

Answers on pages 46-47

Your Grandfather's Bruins

1. When the Bruins were formed, there were five other teams in the NHL. How many of those five hailed from Canada?

2. In the Bruins' first year in the NHL, they set a franchise record for least points recorded in a season. How many points did Boston accrue in their first 30-game season?

   A. 12

   B. 16

   C. 20

   D. 24

3. What year did the Bruins win their first Stanley Cup title?

   A. 1925

   B. 1929

   C. 1935

   D. 1939

4. What year did the Bruins enter the NHL?

   A. 1918

   B. 1924

   C. 1930

   D. 1936

5. What year did the Bruins play their first game at Boston Garden?
   A. 1917-18
   B. 1920-21
   C. 1924-25
   D. 1928-29

6. How much did it cost for the Bruins to originally join the NHL?
   A. $500
   B. $5,000
   C. $15,000
   D. $50,000

7. From which team did the Bruins acquire Phil Esposito?
   A. Chicago Blackhawks
   B. New York Rangers
   C. Montreal Canadiens
   D. Toronto Maple Leafs

8. As World War II raged in Europe, the Bruins had a line of future Hall of Famers with German names. This trio from Kitchener, Ontario of Milt Schmidt, Woody Dumart and Bobby Bauer was affectionately known by what derogatory name?

9. December 21, 1937, marked the first time one brother scored against another in an NHL game as the Bruins faced the Blackhawks. What was the name of the family in which the early puck-sized Christmas present was given?

A. Esposito

B. Patrick

C. Schmidt

D. Thompson

10. This legendary center wrote to the league in 1943 to have an assist taken away, eventually costing him both a scoring title and assist record. Who was this honest Bruin?

A. Dit Clapper

B. Bill Cowley

C. Milt Schmidt

D. Eddie Shore

11. Which Bruin held the NHL record for 37 years with his 1.97 points per game average of 1943-44?

A. Dit Clapper

B. Bill Cowley

C. Milt Schmidt

D. Eddie Shore

12. Whose three overtime goals in the 1939 playoffs forever earned him the nickname "Sudden Death"?

A. Roy Conacher

B. Dit Clapper

C. Mel Hill

D. Milt Schmidt

13. This Hall of Famer was both the first Bruins captain and the first player in NHL history to have his number retired. Who was he?

    A. Marty Barry

    B. Lionel Hitchman

    C. Duke Keats

    D. Eddie Shore

14. What was the team-high in goals in Boston's first season of existence?

    A. 7

    B. 12

    C. 17

    D. 22

15. Pandemonium reigned when the cheap seats went on sale the first night the Bruins played at Boston Garden on November 20, 1928. How cheap was cheap in 1928?

    A. 50 cents

    B. $1.25

    C. $1.75

    D. $2.50

16. The Bruins had the first player to wear protective head gear. Who was this Harvard grad and forward-thinking Bruin?

    A. Dit Clapper

    B. Lionel Hitchman

    C. George Owen

    D. Tiny Thompson

17. Sixty-five years before the Red Sox came back from a 3-0 deficit against the Yankees in the fabled 2004 Championship Series, the Bruins and Rangers went seven games in the Stanley Cup finals after the Bruins had won the first three. Who won this Boston-New York epic?

18. True or false? The Bruins were the first American team to win the Stanley Cup.

19. True or false? When the NHL separated into American and Canadian Divisions in 1926-27, the Bruins won the first American Division title.

20. Who was the first Bruin to win the NHL scoring title?
    A. Dit Clapper
    B. Harry Oliver
    C. Eddie Shore
    D. Cooney Weiland

Answers on pages 47-49

The Original Six

1. The Boston Bruins are one of the "Original Six" hockey teams that date before World War II. The Montreal Canadiens are the only remaining competitor who played the Bruins in their first year of existence. Name the four other "original" teams.

2. Which Bruin was the first American NHL player elected to the Hockey Hall of Fame?

3. In the summer of 1959 the Bruins embarked on a landmark 23-game tour of Europe. Which "Original Six" team accompanied the Bruins?

4. The NHL color barrier was broken by Bruins African-American Willie O'Ree in what year?
   A. 1948
   B. 1958
   C. 1968
   D. 1978

5. During Montreal's untouchable 10 straight years in the Stanley Cup finals (1951-60), how many times did they face the Bruins?

6. True or false? When the NHL doubled in size overnight to a dozen teams in 1967-68, only one team in the newly-minted West Division had a .500 record.

Answers on pages 49-50

Bruins Answers

Bruins Basics

1. D. Adam Oates. He had two goals and two assists in a 4-2 win in Game 4 of the first round of the 1996 playoffs against Florida. It avoided a sweep and was the only win by Boston in the 1996 postseason.

2. C. 1972. The 2011 Bruins won the Stanley Cup for the first time in 39 years. The 1972 win, though, had been their second Cup in three years.

3. Rene Rancourt. The Natick resident won an opera contest in the 1970s heard by Boston Garden and Fenway Park organist John Kiley. Rancourt filled in for Kate Smith for fabled Game 6 of the 1975 World Series and sang the anthem at his first Bruins game the following year. His signature first pump was picked up from former Bruin Randy Burridge.

4. Boston defeated Montreal in the Eastern Conference quarterfinals, 4-2; knocked off the Flyers in the semifinals, 4-0; defeated Tampa Bay in the conference finals, 4-3; and rallied to beat the Canucks for the Stanley Cup, 4-3.

5. C. 15. After the 2003-04 season, a yearlong strike wiped out the 2004-05 season, not to mention ties, as a new agreement went into effect.

6. C. 30. This remarkable streak ran from the 1966-67 season to 1996-97, when the Bruins finished with the worst record in hockey at 26-47-9.

7. The Adams Division. Named for Bruins founder Charles Francis Adams, it was formed in 1974 and existed through 1993, when it became the Northeast Division.

8. Nine. The Bruins went to the playoffs as the top team from the Adams Division in 1976, 1977, 1978, 1979, 1983, 1984, 1990, 1991 and 1993.

9. D. University of Vermont. The UVM alum helped the school to its first-ever Frozen Four appearance in 1996. Overall, Thomas was 81–43–15 with a 2.70 goal against average and .924 save percentage, ranking third in Division I with 3,950 saves.

10. Quebec Nordiques. The Nordiques chose Tim Thomas with the 217th pick in 1994, but he remained in school and did not play in the NHL until 2002 with the Bruins, eight years after being drafted by the Nordiques (who moved to Colorado in 1995). In the interim he bounced around the minors and spent enough time playing in Finland to learn the language.

11. C. 2007-08. Claude Julien, who'd coached previously with the Canadiens and Devils, took over the Bruins in 2007-08 and took them to the playoffs after they'd failed to qualify the previous year.

12. True. Through 2010-11, the Bruins and Canadiens had faced each other 33 times in the playoffs, which to date was 10 more times than the Red Wings and Maple Leafs.

13. Canadiens. Les Habitants hold a 24-9 lead in postseason play against the Bruins.

14. C. 27. The Bruins had been 0-27 in series in which they trailed two games to none before rallying against Montreal in the first round in the 2011 playoffs. The Bruins lost the first two games at home but won Games 5 and 7 in overtime in Boston.

15. A. 8. The Bruins went from 1959-60 to 1966-67 without reaching the playoffs. The club then embarked on a far more impressive streak.

16. C. 1991. Back when the playoffs were a best-of-five, the Canadiens won Game 5 in 1931. They took Game 7 from Boston in 1952, 1971 and 1979 before finally knocking off the Habs in Game 7 in 1991. The teams have gone 2-2 in Game 7 in the 20 years since then, but the Bruins knocked off Montreal in Game 7 on the road to the Stanley Cup in 2011.

17. A. Colorado Avalanche. Ray Bourque, who was traded to the Avalanche late in the 2000 season, won the Stanley Cup in his final career game in 2001.

18. C. Nathan Horton. Though Michael Ryder scored an overtime goal to win Game 4, Horton scored the OT winner in both Games 5 and 7 against Montreal.

19. D. Phoenix Coyotes. The Bruins knocked off the Coyotes by scores of 5-2 and 3-0. It was just like being at home for Slovakian-born Bruins captain Zdeno Chara and Czech teammate David Krejci.

20. B. Philadelphia Flyers. The Bruins rallied to beat Philly with a late goal by Marc Recchi and an overtime winner by Marco Strum.

21. B. Dit Clapper. He played on the first three Cup championship teams in Bruins history: 1929, 1939 and 1941.

22. C. Milt Schmidt. Mr. Boston Bruin played on two Stanley Cup championship teams in the 1939 and 1941 and was general manager of two more Bruins champions in the 1970s. Schmidt was employed by the Bruins in five different decades (1936-72).

23. C. 9 feet. Boston Garden was built in 1928 by boxing promoter Tex Rickard to put fans close enough to "see the sweat on the boxer's face." The NHL had no standard size for rinks in the 1920s. The Garden's 191-foot long, 85-foot wide ice surface fell short of the later NHL ideal of 200 feet long and 85 feet across. The benches and penalty boxes were also different than most arenas. Talk about home ice advantage!

24. C. Edmonton Oilers. The game was tied 3-3 in the second period when the Boston Garden lights went out and could not be restored. The Bruins, down three games to none, got a respite, but two days later the Oilers completed the sweep.

25. C. Eddie Johnston. He played every game of the 1963-64 season, being out on the ice for all 70 games and 4,200 minutes of a brutal 18-40-12 season. The concept of backup goalies—not to mention goalie masks—was late in coming.

26. Mark Recchi. And he followed through on his word, ending his career after his third Stanley Cup triumph as fourth best in NHL history in games (1,652) and in the top 20 all-time in goals (557), assists (956) and points.

27. Johnny Bucyk. The 2011-12 season was his 55th in the employee of the Bruins, though "Chief" is best known for his club record 21 seasons and 545 goals while wearing the spoked "B" crest. He claimed his first two Cups in the 1970s before clocking in number three in 2011.

28. #1 and #6. Everything else is taken: #2 Eddie Shore, #3 Lionel Hitchman, #4 Bobby Orr, #5 Dit Clapper, #7 Phil Esposito, #8 Cam Neely, and #9 Johnny Bucyk.

29. A. Ray Bourque. Bourque's 19 straight appearances in NHL history passed Wayne Gretzky's 18 and was second only to Gordie Howe's 23 overall.

30. #30. Gerry Cheevers was a stick-handling goalie who fit the pace of the 1970s Bruins and ended a 29-year Stanley Cup drought in Boston. A puck stopper and acrobat, Tim Thomas took the Bruins to their first Stanley Cup in 39 years.

31. Ray Bourque. In one of the classiest moves in Bruins history, Ray Bourque, team captain, and the game's best defenseman, surrendered his jersey to Phil Esposito during an on-ice celebration at Boston Garden on December 3, 1987. Bourque wore #77 the rest of his long career; and it now hangs in the rafters at TD Garden.

32. Phil Esposito (#7), Bobby Orr (#4), Milt Schmidt (#15), and Eddie Shore (#2). A fifth, Bill Cowley, would be included in this august circle if the Bruins retired his #10.

33. A. Gerry Cheevers. And he only made it two-thirds of the way through a fifth season. The Bruins goaltending great took over in 1980-81 and was relieved late in 1984-85 in favor of GM Harry Sinden, who finished out the year on the bench and got the Bruins to the conference semifinals—just like Cheevers the year before.

34. C. Eddie Johnston. As Boston's goalie he won 180 regular-season games, good for fourth in Bruins history. Johnston coached the Penguins and served as GM when Lemieux was drafted first overall in 1984. He spent more than a quarter century with the Pittsburgh front office and was also GM, though less successfully, with the Hartford Whalers.

35. C. Harvard. Peter Chiarelli played at Harvard (1983-87) and served as captain before playing professionally in England. A lawyer and agent in Ottawa, he later served as assistant GM with the Senators before joining Boston.

36. Don Sweeney. Assistant GM Sweeney spent 15 years in a Bruins uniform. He played 1,052 games as a Bruins defenseman. Sweeney played with Bruins GM Peter Chiarelli at Harvard.

37. Garnett "Ace" Bailey. A two-time winner of the Stanley Cup with the Bruins, he later took teenaged rookie Wayne Gretzky under his wing in Edmonton and became a scout for the champion Oilers. He was head of pro scouting for the Kings en route to Los Angeles when his plane, Flight 175, was hijacked and crashed into the World Trade Center. His family founded the Ace Bailey Children Foundation in his honor.

38. 1969. January of '69 was a perfect month for the Bruins, led by the Cashman-Esposito-Hodge line. In November 2011 the defending champion Bruins took points in all 13 games in November and outscored opponents, 59-25.

39. Tampa Bay Lightning. After being shelled in a 5-4 loss in Game 6, Tim Thomas saved all 24 shots in a 1-0 win in Game 7—his second shutout of the series—to advance to the Stanley Cup finals.

40. B. Mike Milbury. The longtime Bruins defenseman, who took over from former teammate Terry O'Reilly, guided Boston to its second Stanley Cup final in three years in 1990. Unfortunately, the result was the same: a loss to the powerhouse Edmonton Oilers.

41. B. Pete Peeters. In 1982-83, his first season as a Bruin, Peeters put together a 40-11-9 mark and led the NHL with eight shutouts and just 2.36 goals allowed per game. The New York Islanders dynasty snuffed out Boston's dreams in the conference finals.

42. A. Gerry Cheevers. Cheesy played 88 playoff games for the Bruins, winning 53 (another Bruins record). As if his case as top Bruins netminder needed more evidence, he also coached the Bruins in 34 playoff games, winning 15.

43. A. Gerry Cheevers, Eddie Johnston. This pair split time pretty evenly during the regular season, though Cheevers played more in the playoffs. Both could handle the stick. Johnston set the Bruins record with four assists in 1971-72. Cheevers matched the number in 1976-77.

44. B. Ron Hextall. With the Bruins having yanked the goaltender for an extra skater trailing 4-2 in the closing minutes, the Flyers goaltender, a lefty shooter, by the way, flipped the puck from his goal line, and it clanged into the net. Billy Smith had been credited with a 1979 goal, but this was the first time a goalie scored on a shot on goal.

45. False. In fact the Bruins were the first American team to earn the Presidents' Trophy. Edmonton and Calgary received the award twice each before the Bruins earned the 1990 trophy. It only went so far as they were knocked off by Edmonton in the Stanley Cup finals. It was Boston's only Presidents' Trophy through 2011.

46. B. New Jersey Devils. The end came quickly at the Boston Garden in the 1995 playoffs. The Bruins lost to eventual Stanley Cup champs, 3-2, in Game 5 of the first round of the playoffs. Boston was shut out by Martin Brodeur in its three other losses.

47. C. New York Islanders. The Bruins faced the Islanders in the first regular-season game at the new building on October 7, 1995. It was an ambivalent beginning: a 4-4 tie.

48. 1988. That year the Edmonton Oilers got in 94 fights. They were no match for the NHL-high 132 fights by the '88 Bruins, but the Oilers did spank Boston in the finals.

49. He's 6-foot-9. Zdeno Chara also weighs 255 pounds. That's 2.057 meters and 115.67 kilograms back home.

50. False. Through 2011 Minnesota had produced 216 players. Massachusetts was second with 168.

Fight Night

1. D. Shawn Thornton. The 2010 brawl was the first fight in the three New Year's Day Winter Classics held to that point. Philadelphia's Daniel Carcillo got the better of the punches, and Thornton hit the ice.

2. D. Maurice "Rocket" Richard was suspended for the rest of the season *and* the playoffs following a March 13, 1955 incident at the Boston Garden. Bruins defenseman Hal Laycoe, a former Montreal teammate, high-sticked Richard, leading to the ugly ref-decking. The suspension resulted in a riot in Montreal when NHL president Colin Campbell attended a Canadiens-Red Wings game on March 17.

3. B. Madison Square Garden. Two days before Christmas 1979 at MSG, several Bruins went into the stands after a fan grabbed a Boston stick at the end of a game with the Rangers. As Rangers announcer Jim Gordon said seconds after the first Bruin scaled the glass and jumped into the stands, "Oh, this is going to be bad." It was.

4. B. "Mad Mike" Milbury took off the fan's shoe and hit him with it (twice) before throwing the shoe onto the ice at Madison Square Garden.

5. B. Minnesota North Stars. (They later dropped the "North" and moved to Dallas.) The North Stars had lost 35 straight games at Boston Garden (0-28-7), but they went on to sweep the Bruins that year in the playoffs and made it to the 1981 finals.

6. D. 392 minutes. Yes, 392 minutes, or the amount of time it would take to play six-and-a-half games.

7. A. The first fight broke out seven seconds into the game. Twelve penalties were assessed in the opening seconds. There would be 72 more over the course of the game.

8. C. 12. A dozen men were ejected in the first 20 minutes, five of them Bruins.

Your Father's Bruins

1. Bruce and Keith Crowder. Bruce later served as head coach at UMass-Lowell before taking over at Northeastern. Keith was a 30-goal scorer three times for the Bruins.

2. A. California Golden Seals. Though they played three time zones away, the Seals—owned by Oakland A's maverick Charlie O. Finley—were in the same division as the Bruins for two years. The Seals then became the Cleveland Barons, who subsequently merged with the Minnesota North Stars, who subsequently became the Dallas Stars. Got it?

3. D. 12. The Division winners received byes for the first round until 1978-79, but the following year the top 16 teams made the playoffs regardless of conference.

4. B. 1980. Ray Bourque was voted the league's top rookie during the 1979-80 season. At age 19, the future Hall of Famer scored 17 goals and had 48 assists, and he added 11 more points in the playoffs.

5. B. Ken Dryden. The Bruins took Dryden with the 14th overall pick in the 1964 amateur draft, but he was immediately traded by Boston to Montreal with Alex Campbell for Paul Reid and Guy Allen. Dryden did not even know he'd been originally picked by the Bruins until more than a decade later.

6. A. Garnet "Ace" Bailey beat Rangers goalie Ed Giacomin to win the opener of the 1972 Stanley Cup finals. The Bruins

went on to win the Cup in six games and provide fodder for those "1940" chants reminding Rangers fans when they won their last Stanley Cup.

7. C. The names of every player had appeared on the Cup previously. A veteran team, most of the players had played on the 1970 Cup-champion Bruins or had come from teams that had previously won, including Mike Walton with 1966 champ Toronto.

8. Phil Esposito (152 points), Bobby Orr (139), Johnny Bucyk (116), and Ken Hodge (105).

9. D. Derek Sanderson. Though Gerry Cheevers and John McKenzie also hopped to the upstart World Hockey Association after the 1972 Stanley Cup win, Sanderson received a $2.6 million contract, more than international soccer superstar Pele was making at the time. Sanderson and the Philadelphia Blazers stumbled, and he was bought out for $1 million. He returned to the Bruins but was traded to the Rangers a year later.

10. C. Tom Johnson. Harry Sinden left after the 1970 Stanley Cup title. Johnson, the assistant GM, stepped in as a rookie head coach and Boston didn't miss a beat. The 1971 Bruins set a club record with 57 wins and won the Cup again in 1972, Johnson's eighth time on the trophy (six as a player in Montreal and as a Boston executive in 1970).

11. Brad Park. Considered the best defenseman in the game next to Bobby Orr, the hated Ranger was sent to the Bruins with Jean Ratelle and Joe Zanussi for Phil Esposito and defenseman Carol Vadnais on November 7, 1975. Park's 1972 autobiography, *Play the Man*, had unkind words for Boston Garden, but the Hall of Famer became beloved there and helped the Bruins reach two Stanley Cup finals.

12. B. Montreal Canadiens. The Habs excelled at spoiling the 1970s for the Bruins, starting with knocking out the defending champs in the quarterfinals (when just eight teams made the playoffs). Montreal won the last two games, including Game 7 in Boston, to spoil a 57-win season by the Bruins. Montreal beat the Blackhawks for the Cup.

13. B. 18. It is the smallest number of any Stanley Cup-winning team in the post-expansion era of 1967-68.

14. A. Gary Doak. The defenseman was taken by the Vancouver Canucks in the 1970 expansion draft and traded the following

year to the Rangers, who lost to the Bruins in the 1972 Stanley Cup finals. Doak returned to Boston in 1973 and played in two more finals, though on the losing end.

15. D. 18. Phil Esposito's 76 goals blew away Blackhawk Bobby Hull's mark of 58 set just two years earlier. His 152 points was also a record until Wayne Gretzky came along.

16. Coach Don Cherry got the ax because of a third-period penalty for too many men on the ice at the Montreal Forum. The volatile Cherry and general manager Harry Sinden already had a running feud, and when the Bruins lost their chance to end Montreal's dynasty after leading in the third period, it was the last straw.

17. Bobby Orr in 1967 and Derek Sanderson in 1968. Sanderson, a center and faceoff specialist, was integral in feeding the prodigious scoring defenseman Orr and producing two Stanley Cups for the Bruins.

18. B. Conn Smythe Trophy. Boston's Bobby Orr was the first multiple winner, in 1970 and 1972. First presented in 1965, the trophy honors Smythe, the former owner, GM, and coach of the Toronto Maple Leafs, which explains why the trophy has such a Maple Leaf look to it. (Ironically, through 2011, only one Maple Leaf had ever won it.)

19. Phil Esposito. He led everyone with 13 points in the legendary series with four games in Canada and four in the U.S.S.R. Espo scored the first goal of the series, and his shot in the final minute resulted in a rebound put home by Paul Henderson in Game 8 to give Canada the series, 4-3-1.

20. Phil Esposito and Johnny Bucyk. Espo scored 76 and the Chief netted 51 as the Bruins lit the lamp a staggering 399 times, 108 more goals than any NHL team.

The Bobby Orr Challenge

1. #4. The Bruins suited him up in number 27 originally, and then tried to give him number 5, previously worn by star Dit Clapper. Orr chose number 4 and received a standing ovation in his debut on October 19, 1966.

2. D. All of the above. Agent Alan Eagleson negotiated Bobby Orr's landmark contract, with a $25,000 signing bonus and an annual salary that remained a secret yet still blew any player-negotiated contract out of the water. Speaking of which, the 1966 contract was signed aboard the *Barbara Lynn*,

a boat owned by Bruins GM Hap Emms.

3. D. St. Louis Blues. St. Louis defenseman Noel Picard was the bad sport who committed the trip, but it made for one memorable photo by Ray Lussier.

4. True. Bobby Orr was the first defenseman to ever win a scoring title. Twice. He scored 120 points in 1969-70, practically doubling his previous record for defensemen, and he scored 135 points to lead the NHL in 1974-75.

5. Wayne Gretzky and Mario Lemieux. Gretzky recorded 100 assists an amazing 11 times, while Mario Lemieux did it once, in 1988-89. Bobby Orr's 102 assists came in the 1970-71 season. Give yourself extra credit if you answered Andre Lacroix, who recorded 106 assists for the World Hockey Association's San Diego Mariners in 1974-75.

6. C. Larry Robinson. The Montreal defenseman set the mark for being on the ice for 730 more goals than allowed. At age 34 Robinson took over a mark Bobby Orr had held since he was 20. Boston's Ray Bourque ended up third all-time with 528.

7. A. Chicago Blackhawks. Orr's agent Alan Eagleson withheld information from him about getting a piece of Bruins ownership in 1980, and he colluded to strike a deal with Chicago before the free agency period started. Orr played just 26 games in three years with the Blackhawks.

8. A. 31. And that was after playing just 36 games in his final four years.

Your Grandfather's Bruins

1. Five. The other five NHL teams were all from Canada (in order of finish): Toronto St. Patricks, Montreal Canadiens, Hamilton Tigers, Ottawa Senators and Montreal Maroons.

2. A. 12. The Bruins finished with just 12 points, and no other Bruins team has ever come within 26 points of that dismal mark. The original Bruins finished with a 6-24 record and a miserable 119 goals allowed compared to just 49 goals scored.

3. B. 1929. Just five seasons after joining the NHL, the Bruins won their first Stanley Cup in Cy Denneny's only season as Bruins coach. A Hall of Fame player, Denneny, 37, also saw time as left wing with the champion Bruins of 1929.

4. B. 1924. The only other "Original Six" team that survived was the Montreal Canadiens. The Toronto St. Patricks, which was

later sold and became the Maple Leafs in 1927, was also in the league in 1924.

5. D. 1928-29. And it was considered akin to attending the theater, with men and women dressed in finery to watch the Bruins dominate in their early years at the Garden.

6. C. $15,000. With the "Roaring Twenties" in full swing, grocery store magnate Charles F. Adams plunked down that sum to join the NHL and become the league's first American franchise.

7. A. Chicago Blackhawks. The center for the great Bobby Hull, Espo was among the league's top scorers when he was traded to the Bruins with Ken Hodge and Fred Stanfield in1967. The trio became stars in Boston as the Bruins became darlings of the city and Esposito became a legendary scoring machine.

8. The Kraut Line. They joined the Royal Canadian Air Force as a trio after the 1941 season against Germany in World War II.

9. C. Thompson. Paul the Blackhawk scored on older brother Tiny, the legendary Bruins goalie, at Boston Garden in 1937. It was the only goal Chicago scored on his big brother in a 2-1 win. Tiny already owned bragging rights for holding his younger bro scoreless in 1929 when the Bruins beat Paul's Rangers for the Stanley Cup.

10. B. Bill Cowley. On track to break his own NHL record for assists in a season (45), he sent a note to NHL president Red Dutton requesting that an assist erroneously credited to him against the Rangers be taken away. The stunned Dutton complied, and Cowley wound up finishing one point short for both the scoring title and assist record!

11. B. Bill Cowley. Again! Limited to just 36 games because of injury, Cowley still racked up 30 goals and 41 assists for the 1943-44 Bruins. The 1.97 points per game average lasted until Edmonton's Wayne Gretzky notched 2.05 ppg in 1980-81.

12. C. Mel Hill. Though seven Bruins scored more goals during the season, "Sudden Death" Hill tallied three OT goals in the semifinals against the Rangers. Two of those winners came in triple overtime, including the Game 7 clincher. When the Bruins bounced the Maple Leafs for the Stanley Cup, their only loss, ironically, came in OT.

13. B. Lionel Hitchman. A former Royal Canadian Mountie, he was already a Stanley Cup winner (with Ottawa) when the

first-year Bruins acquired him. The Hall of Fame defenseman anchored the team's defense—with Eddie Shore—and Hitchman earned the first captaincy in Bruins history in 1927.

14. A. 17. Thank goodness for Jimmy Herbert, who recorded 17 goals and seven assists for the inaugural Bruins. No one scored more than five times. Lionel Hitchman arrived with just a third of the season gone, but he solidified a defense that was in the midst of a 1-18 skid.

15. A. The cheap seats went for 50 cents on opening night and for all of 1928-29, the season that put the Bruins on the map and on the Stanley Cup.

16. C. George Owen. Though born in Hamilton, Ontario, Owen grew up in Newton and was a hockey legend at Harvard. He went into the bond business after college, but he continued playing amateur hockey. He signed with the Bruins in 1929, doffing the same helmet he'd worn playing football at Harvard.

17. The Bruins. And it wasn't easy. Boston pulled out the victory in double overtime after letting the Rangers back in the 1939 finals. New York would beat Boston in the semifinals the next year and win the Stanley Cup, but even that had a hollow ring that became the "1940" chant that followed Rangers fans until their next Cup in 1994.

18. False. From the time it was donated by Lord Stanley in 1892, the Seattle Metropolitans, a non-National Hockey Association team, beat the Canadiens for the 1917 Cup—a 1919 rematch was cancelled by the flu epidemic. The Bruins had a chance for the first all-NHL Cup in 1926 but lost to Ottawa. The Rangers won it the next year.

19. False. The Rangers won the first American Division title in 1927, though the Bruins won the most American Division titles with seven, while the Red Wings won three and the Rangers two before the NHL reverted to a single six-team league in 1939.

20. D. Cooney Weiland. In 1929-30 his 73 points (43 goals, 30 assists) in 44 games shattered the mark of 51 set two years earlier by Montreal's Howie Morenz. Weiland's mark would stand until 1944, when it was broken by Bruin Herb Cain.

The Original Six

1. Chicago Blackhawks, Detroit Red Wings, New York Rangers,

and Toronto Maple Leafs. There were as many as 10 NHL teams in the 1920s, but the Depression and the manpower shortage caused by Canada's entry into World War II with England in 1939 led to the league being whittled down to six clubs in 1942.

2. Frank Brimsek. The legendary goalie and Minnesota native broke the monopoly of Canadian-born NHL players in the Hockey Hall of Fame when he was honored in Toronto in 1966. The U.S. Hall of Fame inducted the Bruins great in 1973.

3. New York Rangers. The Canadiens refused to go on one plane across the ocean for fear that a crash would wipe out their dynasty. When a couple of Ranger players couldn't go, Chicago sent young Bobby Hull to fill out the roster. The Rangers held a slim lead in the series, 11-9-3. Leo Labine of the Bruins was high scorer with 18 goals.

4. B. 1958. Willie O'Ree of New Brunswick, Canada, played parts of two seasons with the Bruins, totaling four goals and 10 assists, all in 1961. He played in the minors until age 43, despite being blind in one eye from being hit with a puck—a condition he kept secret.

5. Three. The Habs won all three in 1953, 1957 and 1958. Only the Detroit Red Wings, who won three Cups between 1951-60, appeared in more finals (four). The Toronto Maple Leafs appeared in the other three Cup finals in that span, winning one. The Canadiens won the rest: six Cups, including the last five from 1956-60.

6. False. No team in the West Division had a winning record. The Philadelphia Flyers came closest at 31-32-11, finishing ahead of the newbie Los Angeles Kings, St. Louis Blues, Minnesota North Stars, Pittsburgh Penguins and Oakland Seals. The Canadiens, who bounced the Bruins in the play-offs, swept the Blues for the Stanley Cup.

The Celltics

2

Celtics Basics

1. What was the flooring at the old Boston Garden called?

2. Name the two Celtics broadcasters who have been working together for more than 30 years.

3. True or false? In Shaquille O'Neal's one year with the Celtics in 2010-11, he put together the highest field-goal percentage of his illustrious career.

4. The 2010-11 Celtics led the NBA in fewest points allowed, but in what significant offensive category did they also lead the league?
   A. Field-goal attempts
   B. Field-goal percentage
   C. Free-throw percentage
   D. Points scored per game

5. Who led the NBA with 189 steals during the 2009-10 campaign?

6. Who is the only Celtics coach to reach the postseason but never win a playoff game for Boston?

    A. John Carroll

    B. Jim O'Brien

    C. Rick Pitino

    D. Jimmy Rodgers

7. True or false? Rick Pitino never had a winning season as coach of the Celtics.

8. Besides serving as head coach of the Celtics, what other hat did Pitino wear with the team?

    A. CEO

    B. General Manager

    C. President

    D. All of the above

9. How many games did the Celtics improve in the standings between the 2006-07 and 2007-08 seasons?

    A. 27 games

    B. 32 games

    C. 37 games

    D. 42 games

10. Name two of the three players sent to Seattle after the 2006-07 season in the franchise-altering deal for Ray Allen, plus Glenn Davis.

11. True or false? Stephon Marbury ended his turbulent career by winning a championship with the Celtics.

12. Who set the record for career three-pointers while wearing a Celtics uniform in 2011?

13. Which Celtic holds the NBA record for most consecutive playoff free throws made, with 56?
    A. Larry Bird
    B. Dave Cowens
    C. Bob Cousy
    D. Bill Sharman

14. What Celtic played with Shaquille O'Neal in Boston at age 25 after having body-slammed Shaq in a wrestling match when he was 15?

15. Who was the only full-time Celtics head coach to have a winning percentage lower than .300?
    A. M.L. Carr
    B. Dave Cowens
    C. Jim O'Brien
    D. Rick Pitino

16. Name Boston's first-round pick of 1986 who tragically died before ever taking the court for the Celtics.

17. Celtics coaches have had some interesting nick-
    names through the years. Try to match their first
    names with their last names.

    A. Doc   1. Julian
    B. Doggie   2. Rivers
    C. Honey   3. Russell
    D. Satch   4. Sanders

18. What major league baseball team did Danny
    Ainge play for while in college before being
    drafted by the Boston Celtics?

    A. Boston Red Sox
    B. New York Yankees
    C. Seattle Mariners
    D. Toronto Blue Jays

19. Who was stabbed 11 times in the face, neck and
    back a month before the 2000-01 season yet did
    not miss a game all year for the Celtics?

20. How much was Celtics president of basketball
    operations Danny Ainge fined for throwing a
    towel during an opponent's free-throw attempt
    during a 2010 playoff game?

    A. $10,000
    B. $15,000
    C. $20,000
    D. $25,000

21. True or false? The 1996-97 Celtics (15-67) had the
    fewest wins in franchise history.

22. True or false? The 2007-08 Celtics had the highest winning percentage (.805) in franchise history.

23. True or false? Boston's four straight first-place finishes from 2007-11 were the most in a row by the franchise since the 1950s.

24. The first two presidents of the NBA Players Association were Celtics stars. Can you name them?

25. Red Auerbach was the first Celtics to coach 100 playoff games. Who was the second?

26. Who joined the roll of Celtics in the Basketball Hall of Fame in 2011?

27. Where is the Basketball Hall of Fame located in Massachusetts?

28. Through 2011, how many men both played for and coached the Celtics?
    A. 3
    B. 5
    C. 7
    D. 9

29. Who was Boston's last player-coach?
    A. Dave Cowens
    B. Tommy Heinsohn
    C. Bill Russell
    D. Satch Sanders

30. Who was the only Celtic voted into the Hall of
    Fame twice—as both a player and a coach?
    A. Red Auerbach
    B. Bob Cousy
    C. Bill Russell
    D. Bill Sharman

31. Which Hall of Famer never played for the Celtics?
    A. Wayne Embry
    B. Cliff Hagan
    C. Bob McAdoo
    D. Andy Phillip

32. Which former Celtics player coached an NCAA
    championship team?
    A. Bob Cousy
    B. K.C. Jones
    C. John Thompson
    D. Paul Westphal

33. Which current or former NBA coach never played
    for the Celtics?
    A. Rick Carlisle
    B. Paul Silas
    C. Dick Vitale
    D. Paul Westphal

34. Which gregarious college basketball coach gave Doc Rivers his nickname as a kid during a basketball camp?

    A. Jim Calhoun

    B. Rick Majerus

    C. Rick Pitino

    D. Dick Vitale

35. Which NBA team did Doc Rivers coach before he took over the Celtics?

    A. Atlanta Hawks

    B. New York Knicks

    C. Orlando Magic

    D. San Antonio Spurs

36. What prompted Boston to fire Jimmy Rodgers after the 1989-90 season, despite a 52-30 record?

37. How many Hall of Famers played for Boston's first championship team in 1957?

38. The Celtics have actually had eight future Hall of Famers on one team in multiple years. How many times?

39. Were Ray Allen and Allan Ray ever on the Celtics at the same time?

40. Who is the only Celtic to win NBA Defensive Player of the Year?

A. Kevin Garnett

B. Kevin McHale

C. Rajon Rondo

D. Bill Russell

41. Who left the floor in a wheelchair in Game 1 of the 2008 NBA finals only to return to the court a few minutes later and lead the Celtics to victory?

42. Who led the team in scoring in the first Celtics season in professional basketball?

A. Chuck Connors

B. Jack Garfinkel

C. Connie Simmons

D. Johnny Simmons

43. What Celtic stopped wearing his signature headband when the NBA suddenly made a 2010 rule forbidding headbands to be worn upside down?

44. When the strike-shortened season started on Christmas Day 2011, what team did the Celtics open up against?

45. The Celtics played select games at the Hartford Civic Center from 1975-95. What was Boston's winning percentage in Connecticut's capital?

A. .438

B. .510

C. .596

D. .697

46. The 2008 NBA title ended a drought of how many years for the Celtics?

A. 18

B. 39

C. 41

D. 86

47. Through 2011, how many NBA championships have the Celtics won?

48. How many different coaches have won championships for the Celtics?

49. The Celtics got their first franchise win and 3,000th win against teams from the same city 65 years apart. What city was it?

A. Chicago

B. New York

C. Philadelphia

D. Toronto

50. The 3,000th win in Celtics history also was the 308th by Doc Rivers with the Celtics, tying him for third place with which Boston coaching great?

A. Red Auerbach

B. Tom Heinsohn

C. K.C. Jones

D. Bill Fitch

Answers on pages 76-81

Your Father's Celtics

1. How many future Hall of Famers were members of the 1986 team?

2. A Celtic was the first player to win the NBA's Sixth Man Award in successive years in the 1980s. Who was he?

3. How many NBA titles did the Celtics win in the 1980s?

4. In one 10-day span in 1985 the club record for points in a game was set by two different players. Who were the two record breakers?

5. Who was voted MVP in Boston's win over the Lakers in the 1968-69 NBA finals?
   A. Em Bryant
   B. John Havlicek
   C. Bill Russell
   D. Jerry West

6. In 1971 the Rookie of the Year Award ended in a tie. Which Celtic got half the award?
   A. Don Chaney
   B. Dave Cowens
   C. Bill Dinwiddie
   D. Jo Jo White

7. M.L. Carr was a shooting guard on two NBA champion Celtics teams in the 1980s and served as general manager and head coach in the 1990s. What does M.L. stand for?

A. Martin Luther

B. Martin Lawrence

C. Michael Leon

D. Morgan Le Fay

8. In a shrewd move just before the 1980 draft, the Celtics traded the first overall selection to Golden State for one future star and then drafted another future star with the Warriors' pick. Name the two future Hall of Famers who came to Boston in Red Auerbach's heist?

9. Which Celtics iron man played in all 82 games for five straight seasons during the 1970s?

A. Dave Cowens

B. Dave Havlicek

C. Paul Silas

D. Jo Jo White

10. What was Robert Parish's nickname?

11. Who did the Celtics beat in triple overtime in Game 5 of the 1976 NBA finals?

A. Golden State Warriors

B. Los Angeles Lakers

C. Phoenix Suns

D. Seattle Supersonics

12. How many future NBA coaches were in uniform for the two teams in legendary Game 5 of the 1976 NBA finals at the Boston Garden?

13. True or false? Bill Russell was the first African American coach in NBA history.

14. Who came to the Celtics in return for Dave Cowens in 1982?
    A. Danny Ainge
    B. Quinn Buckner
    C. Dennis Johnson
    D. Bill Walton

15. Former Celtic Quinn Buckner was drafted by NBA and NFL teams in 1976. The Milwaukee Bucks took him in the first round, but which NFL team chose him as a free safety?
    A. New England Patriots
    B. New York Jets
    C. Tampa Bay Buccaneers
    D. Washington Redskins

16. The 1964-65 Celtics were the first team with a starting five comprised of only African Americans. Name three members of this historic starting five.

17. The year before Boston drafted Larry Bird was the first time the Celtics had finished with fewer than 30 wins since which season?

A. 1949-1950

B. 1954-1955

C. 1969-1970

D. 1977-1978

18. Which team won more consecutive championships: the 1950s and 1960s Celtics or the 1960s and 1970s UCLA men's basketball team?

19. What was John Havlicek's nickname?

20. The 1977-78 Celtics hosted the last game played by the Buffalo Braves before they relocated and renamed themselves the…

A. Bobcats

B. Clippers

C. Jazz

D. Kings

Answers on pages 81-83

The Larry Bird Challenge

1. Larry Bird was taken with the sixth overall pick in the 1978 NBA draft. Which of these players was *not* drafted ahead of him?

   A. Maurice Cheeks

   B. Michael Ray Richardson

   C. Purvis Short

   D. Mychal Thompson

2. What college did Larry Bird attend?

3. Larry Bird was drafted in 1978 but did not play in Boston for another year. Why?

4. True or false? The Celtics only missed the playoffs once during Larry Bird's 13 seasons as a Celtic.

5. Larry Bird scored 12 of the East's last 15 points to beat the West and earn MVP honors in which NBA All-Star Game?

   A. 1982

   B. 1984

   C. 1986

   D. 1988

6. Larry Bird was the third player to win three straight league MVP awards. Name the two legends who achieved it first?

7. True or false? Larry Bird was the only Celtic on the 1992 "Dream Team" at the 1992 Olympics.

Answers on pages 83-84

Your Grandfather's Celtics

1. The Celtics set an NBA record for most points scored in a regulation game on February 27, 1959. How many did they put up?

   A. 158

   B. 165

   C. 173

   D. 181

2. Which professional team drafted Celtics great John Havlicek as a wide receiver?

   A. Boston Patriots

   B. Cleveland Browns

   C. New York Giants

   D. New York Titans

3. In the famous "Havlicek stole the ball" call in the seventh game of the 1965 Eastern Conference finals, who did John Havlicek steal the ball from?

   A. Elgin Baylor

   B. Wilt Chamberlain

   C. Larry Costello

   D. Will Greer

4. Who was the first Celtic to score 1,000 points in a season?

   A. Gene Conley

   B. Bob Cousy

   C. Ed Macauley

   D. Bill Sharman

5. Red Auerbach replaced which Celtics coach?
    A. Honey Russell
    B. Tom Heinsohn
    C. Doggie Julian
    D. Bill Russell

6. What league did the Celtics play in when the team was formed in 1946-47?

7. In 1950 the Celtics became the first NBA team to draft an African American player. Who was he?
    A. Sweetwater Clifton
    B. Chuck Cooper
    C. K.C. Jones
    D. Bill Russell

8. Name the three franchise-changing players acquired by Red Auerbach on the same day in the 1956 NBA draft.

9. Which year did the Celtics win their first world championship?
    A. 1946
    B. 1952
    C. 1957
    D. 1961

10. The Celtics won their first championship in double overtime in Game 7 when a ball rolled around the rim and did not go in at the buzzer. Which team lost this epic battle to the Celtics?

A. Fort Wayne Pistons

B. Minneapolis Lakers

C. St. Louis Hawks

D. Syracuse Nationals

11. Celtics Hall of Fame guard Bill Sharman was an outfielder in the Brooklyn Dodgers system when he set a major league precedent in 1951. What did he do as a Dodger?

A. He was injured warming up and never got into a game.

B. He was ejected from a major league game without ever playing in one.

C. He hit a grand slam his first time up in the majors.

D. He was implicated in the sign-stealing operation at the Polo Grounds.

12. The Celtics had a player on its 1959 championship squad who had already won a World Series in baseball. Who was it?

A. Gene Conley

B. Chuck Connors

C. Rick Reed

D. Bill Sharman

13. How many times did the Celtics win championships with Red Auerbach as coach?

14. How many postseason games did Red Auerbach win as coach of the Celtics?
    A. 70
    B. 80
    C. 90
    D. 100

15. Who was the first Boston Celtic inducted in the Basketball Hall of Fame?
    A. Red Auerbach
    B. Walter Brown
    C. Bob Cousy
    D. Ed Macauley

16. True or false? Celtics legend Bob Cousy averaged significantly more points in the playoffs than the regular season during his career.

17. Which legendary announcer was young Johnny Most hired to replace on Celtics radio broadcasts in 1953?
    A. Marv Albert
    B. Marty Glickman
    C. Curt Gowdy
    D. Chick Hearn

18. True or false? Red Auerbach never played a game in the pros.

19. To which local college did Bob Cousy go to coach after retiring as a Celtic player?

    A. Boston College

    B. Boston University

    C. Suffolk

    D. Tufts

20. True or false? The Celtics drafted Bob Cousy in the first round.

Answers on pages 84-86

The Bill Russell Challenge

1. Celtics legends Bill Russell and K.C. Jones were teammates on two national championship clubs at which university?

   A. Kansas

   B. New York University

   C. UCLA

   D. University of San Francisco

2. Bill Russell did not begin his Celtics career until 16 games into the 1956-57 season. Why?

3. Bill Russell once held the NBA record for rebounds in a game. How many did the big man snag?

   A. 41

   B. 45

   C. 51

   D. 55

4. In the great rivalry between Bill Russell and Wilt Chamberlain, the duo faced each other 191 times in the regular season and playoffs. How often did Bill Russell beat Wilt's teams?

   A. 77

   B. 89

   C. 101

   D. 114

5. Bill Russell was the first basketball player to host what show?

   A. *The Carol Burnett Show*

   B. *The Mike Douglas Show*

   C. *Saturday Night Live*

   D. *The Tonight Show*

6. True or false? Bill Russell is the only player-coach in Celtics history.

7. Bill Russell set a record for most championships won. How many did he claim in his 13-year career as a player?

Answers on pages 86-87

Celtics in the Rafters

1. Number 1 was retired by the Celtics in honor of...
    A. Red Auerbach
    B. Walter Brown
    C. Bob Cousy
    D. Bill Russell

2. Like number 1, number 2 was retired without ever having been worn by a Celtics player. Who was it retired for?

3. Former Celtics coach Bill Fitch once said after a loss to the Clippers, "If I've got anyone in there who doesn't think we played a stinking game, then they've got Robert Parish's number for an IQ?" What number did Parish wear?

4. Number 25 is the only Celtics uniform number between 1 and 99 that has been retired with only one player ever wearing it. Who wore it?
    A. Bob Cousy
    B. Bill Havlicek
    C. K.C. Jones
    D. Bill Sharman

5. What is "MIC" stand for among the list of retired Celtics numbers?

6. What future NBA coaching great served as sixth man for five championship Celtics teams in the 1960s and 1970s and had his number 19 retired at the Boston Garden?

7. Several Celtics uniform numbers continued to be worn by other players only to have the number be retired retroactively. Match the letter with the number that kept on counting even after retirement.

   A. Tom Heinsohn   15
   B. Ed Macauley   21
   C. Cedric Maxwell   22
   D. Bill Sharman   31

8. Through 2011, how many uniform numbers have been retired by the Celtics?
   A. 12
   B. 15
   C. 18
   D. 21

Answers on page 87

Celtics Answers

Celtics Basics

1. Parquet. The red oak panels were probably the most famous sports flooring this side of Home Depot.

2. Mike Gorman and Tommy Heinsohn. The tandem started doing Celtics games on television in 1981.

3. True. Though Shaq led the league in field-goal percentage 10 times, his .667 mark in 2010-11 was the highest of his 19 seasons. His 201 attempts were far fewer than he'd had in past seasons, but it's still pretty accurate for a 38-year-old big man.

4. B. Field-goal percentage. The Celts led the NBA with a .486 field-goal percentage to go with a 91.1 points allowed per game. Put those together and it adds up to 56 wins.

5. Rajon Rondo. The Celtics guard's 189 steals inspired "Grand Theft Rondo" T-shirts.

6. A. John Carroll. He took over after Jim O'Brien (not to be confused with the Ohio State coach of the same name) re-signed due to "philosophical differences" with Boston GM Danny Ainge in January 2004. The Celtics were swept by Indiana that spring, and Carroll was replaced by Doc Rivers.

7. True. Rick Pitino won a division title with the Knicks before leaving to coach Kentucky after the 1988-89 season, but he had no such luck in his return to the pros a decade later with the Celts. Pitino was 102-146 in Boston before resigning in 2001.

8. D. All of the above. It did not work out well.

9. D. 42 games. That staggering turnaround is the biggest in NBA history as the Celts went from 24-win laughingstock to 66 wins and an NBA title.

10. Delonte West, Wally Szcerbiak and Jeff Green. The Celts also shipped the Supersonics a 2008 second-round draft pick.

11. False. Stephon Marbury went out in the second round with the Celtics in the 2009 playoffs, losing to the Magic in seven games. Starbury's 12 points (against Orlando) and 13 points (against Chicago) exceeded any point total he had in his 23 games during the season.

12. Ray Allen. On February 10, 2011, Allen broke Reggie Miller's record of 2,560 three-pointers, which had stood for 13 years.

13. D. Bill Sharman. Sharman helped the Celtics claim four NBA titles between 1957 and 1961. He is one of only three men inducted into the Basketball Hall of Fame as both a player and a coach.

14. Glenn "Big Baby" Davis. At a basketball camp at Louisiana State University, the 15-year-old Davis was challenged to a wrestling match by LSU alum Shaquille O'Neal. Davis got the better of Shaq. Baton Rouge's Big Baby wound up going to LSU and in 2006 led the Tigers to their first Final Four in 20 years.

15. A. M.L. Carr, who coached the Celtics from 1995-97, went just 48-116 for a .293 winning percentage.

16. Len Bias. He died from a cocaine overdose 48 hours after being taken with the second pick in 1986 out of the University of Maryland.

17. A-2: Doc Rivers, B-1: Doggie Julian, C-3: Honey Russell, D-4: Satch Sanders.

18. D. Toronto Blue Jays. Danny Ainge played mostly second and third base for the Blue Jays in 1979-81. He batted .220 and hit two home runs in 211 games before going into pro basketball as Boston's second-round pick out of Brigham Young University in 1981. After a legal battle, the Celtics had to buy out his contract from the Blue Jays.

19. Paul Pierce. He was stabbed on September 25, 2000 at a Boston dance club called Buzz Club. Witnesses say he was trying to break up a fight. Pierce was the only Celtic to play all 81 games in 2000-01 and averaged 25.3 points per game.

20. D. $25,000. "That's a lot of towels," joked Boston coach Doc Rivers. Danny Ainge tossed a towel in the air during Cavalier J.J. Hickson's second free throw in Game 2 of the 2010 Eastern

Conference semifinals. The Celtics had been winning by 23 points in the third quarter at the time. They won by 18.

21. True. Sadly. Even the moribund Celtics of strike-shortened 1998-99 won four more games than M.L. Carr's sorry group of three years earlier. In the struggling early years of the franchise, with fewer dates on the schedule, the Celts still won at least 20.

22. False. The 2007-08 Celtics went 66-16, for an .805 win percentage. That is shy of the 67-15 Celts of 1985-86 and their .817 percentage. Both those clubs won championships, but the Celtics team with the best regular-season mark, the 68-14 (.829) club of 1972-73, lost in the conference finals.

23. False. The Celtics of 1983-88 and 1971-76 won five straight division titles. The mother of all Celtics first-place streaks ran nine straight seasons, 1956-65.

24. Bob Cousy and Tommy Heinsohn. Cousy was a founding member and Heinsohn helped bring in free agency by threatening to strike the 1964 All-Star Game.

25. K.C. Jones. He actually had a better postseason winning percentage than Red Auerbach (.637 to .608), but Red coached 46 more playoff games, and his 90 postseason wins are 25 more than his protégé.

26. Tom (Satch) Sanders. The former Celts player and coach was inducted as a contributor. The NYU grad and former Harvard coach also developed the NBA Rookie Transition Program at Northeastern, a prototype for professional leagues everywhere.

27. Springfield. This western Massachusetts city is where James Naismith invented the game in 1891 at the International YMCA Training School in Springfield. The Hall of Fame opened in 1959 at Springfield College, the site of the former YMCA training school, before opening its own facility in 1985.

28. C. 7: M.L. Carr, Dave Cowens, Chris Ford, Tommy Heinsohn, K.C. Jones, Bill Russell, and Satch Sanders.

29. A. Dave Cowens. He was player-coach for part of 1978-79 but then returned to being solely a player the following year.

30. D. Bill Sharman. He also played minor league baseball, but he was a major force with the Celtics from 1951-61. A flawless free-throw shooter, he was a perfect compliment to Bob Cousy

on four championship teams. After retiring as a player, he was Coach of the Year in both the ABA and NBA and won titles in both leagues.

31. Cliff Hagan. Though originally drafted out of Kentucky by the Celtics, he spent two years in military service and was traded to the St. Louis Hawks before ever playing in the NBA. It worked out all right for the Celtics, who got the rights to Bill Russell in the deal.

32. C. John Thompson. A power forward out of Providence College, Thompson played for the 1964-66 Celtics and coached Georgetown to the NCAA title in 1984.

33. C. Dick Vitale. He started coaching at 20 at an elementary school, worked his way to high school, college (Rutgers and University of Detroit) and the pros. He coached the Pistons for two years before his firing in 1979. It was the best thing that ever happened to him. A fledgling sports network named ESPN came calling, and the talking never stopped.

34. B. Rick Majerus. Majerus, then an assistant at Marquette, spotted Glenn Anton Rivers wearing a "Dr. J" T-shirt during a 1970s basketball camp and started calling him "Doc." So did everyone else. And Rivers wound up playing for Majerus at Marquette.

35. C. Orlando Magic. Doc Rivers played for the Hawks, Knicks and Spurs (plus the Clippers), but his lone head coaching job before arriving in Boston was in Orlando (1998-2004), where he won Coach of the Year in 2000.

36. The Celtics lost in the first round of the playoffs. Not just that, but Boston lost the best-of-five playoff series to the New York Knicks after winning the first two games. That'll get you fired.

37. Six: Bob Cousy, Tom Heinsohn, Andy Phillip, Frank Ramsey, Bill Russell, and Bill Sharman. Plus they were owned by Walter Brown and coached by Red Auerbach, two more Hall of Famers.

38. Three times. 1961: Bob Cousy, Tom Heinsohn, K.C. Jones, Sam Jones, Frank Ramsey, Bill Russell, Bill Sharman, and Tom Sanders. 1963: same, except John Havlicek instead of Sharman. 1964: same as '63 except Clyde Lovelette in place of Cousy.

39. No. There was a Tony Allen on the 2006-07 Celtics with Allan Ray, but when Ray Allen landed in Boston a year later, Allan Ray was on his way to play in Europe.

40. A. Kevin Garnett. The Defensive Player of the Year Award, given out since 1982-83, finally went to a Celtic in 2007-08, his first season with the team.

41. Paul Pierce. Pierce injured his knee in the opener against the Lakers, leaving the court in serious pain and in a wheelchair. He soon returned and pumped in 15 points that same quarter as the Celts won, 98-88. Pierce was MVP of the finals.

42. C. Connie Simmons. Connie, younger brother of Johnny, scored 620 points, 10.3 points per game, as Boston's first starting center. Unlike Johnny, an NYU man, Connie did not attend college. At least they had each other on the inaugural 22-38 Celtics, who tied for last in the division with Toronto.

43. Rajon Rondo. The NBA had earlier forced players to only use an NBA-sanctioned headband. With Rondo being probably the most visible wearer of headbands—and preferring to wear his upside down—the sudden rule against the little logo NBA man appearing upside down ended the Rondo headwear era.

44. New York Knicks, who won a 106-104 nailbiter. After a basketball strike trimmed the 2011 portion of 2011-12 to one week, the NBA opened the season with a series of gifts that included Celtics-Knicks. The present must have said, "Do not open the season until Christmas."

45. D. .697. The Celtics were an impressive 46-20 in 66 games in Hartford over a 20-year span before keeping the game in Boston for good. It may have been in another state, but that nearly .700 winning percentage made it feel just like home.

46. A. 18. As far as Boston droughts go, it was pretty minor next to the slumps ended in the 2000s by the Bruins (39 years), Patriots (41) and Red Sox (86).

47. 17. It's a number every Celtics fan should know and cherish.

48. Six. Red Auerbach, Bill Russell, Tom Heinsohn, Bill Fitch, K.C. Jones and Doc Rivers.

49. D. Toronto. On November 16, 1946, the victim was the Toronto Huskies at Boston Garden, 53-49. On January 11, 2011, it was the Toronto Raptors, with both teams more than doubling the score of the original, 122-102. Shows what progress, a three-point stripe and a shot clock can do.

50. K.C. Jones. Doc Rivers tied—and the next night surpassed—the 308 wins by K.C. Jones. Rivers had already passed Bill Fitch (242) and trailed Tom Heinsohn (427) and Red Auerbach (795).

Your Father's Celtics

1. Five: Larry Bird, Dennis Johnson, Kevin McHale, Robert Parrish and Bill Walton.

2. Kevin McHale. Shortly after the Sixth Man Award was adopted, McHale won it in 1983-84 and 1984-85 for the Celtics. Bill Walton won it for Boston the next year.

3. Three: 1981, 1984 and 1986.

4. Kevin McHale and Larry Bird. McHale recorded 56 against Detroit on March 3. Bird broke that mark with 60 points just 10 days later against Atlanta.

5. D. Jerry West. West averaged 38 points per game against Boston in the finals, including a 42-point effort in Game 7. Celtics player-coach Bill Russell sought out West and embraced him after the game.

6. B. Dave Cowens. He played 81 games and was Boston's third-leading scorer, though he led the team in rebounds by a wide margin. He shared Rookie of the Year with Geoff Petrie of Portland. It marked the start of a long brilliant career for Cowens.

7. C. Michael Leon. He grew up in rural North Carolina and attended tiny Guilford College in his native state. Originally cut in the ABA, he played in Israel before returning to the U.S. in the ABA and eventually winding up with the Celtics.

8. Robert Parish and Kevin McHale. Golden State wanted Joe Barry Carroll and traded Parish and the third overall pick for the top spot in the draft. Though McHale held out after being drafted, he made the All-Rookie team and became a valuable and beloved player in Boston, as did Parish. Both wound up in the Hall of Fame.

9. D. Jo Jo White. He played all 82 games from 1972-73 to 1976-77, averaging about 40 minutes per game. He also played in seven straight all-star games for Boston.

10. "Chief." Cedric Maxwell gave Parish the nickname because of a resemblance to the massive and silent fictional Native

American by that name in the acclaimed film *One Flew Over the Cuckoo's Nest*.

11. C. Phoenix Suns. In one of the wildest games ever, fans were on the court during play at the end of the second overtime after the referees brought the seemingly victorious Celtics out of the locker room for two more seconds. Phoenix almost made another miracle comeback in the third overtime, but the Celts held on, 128-126.

12. Eight future NBA head coaches: Dave Cowens, Garfield Heard, Don Nelson, Pat Riley, Paul Silas, Dick Van Arsdale, Paul Westphal and John Wetzel.

13. True. Bill Russell's ascendancy in 1966-67 made him the first in any major American sports league—Frank Robinson integrated the baseball manager's office with Cleveland in 1975, and Art Shell did it for football in 1990 (though Fritz Pollard served as a co-coach in 1921 in the league that was forerunner to the NFL).

14. B. Quinn Buckner. The Celtics received the solid defender from the Milwaukee Bucks before the 1982-83 season for Dave Cowens, who came out of retirement and would quit for good after the season. Buckner was the key "sixth man" in Boston's 1984 NBA championship.

15. D. Washington Redskins. Washington chose Quinn Buckner in the 14th round with the 393rd pick—he had played two years in Indiana's defensive backfield. Defense was his specialty with the Hoosiers, and Bob Knight named him captain as a sophomore. As a senior he led Indiana to a 32-0 record and the national championship.

16. K.C. Jones, Sam Jones, Tom "Satch" Sanders, Willie Naulls and Bill Russell. This fivesome started, and won, 12 straight games between December 26, 1964 and January 20, 1965, when Tom Heinsohn came back from an injury. The Celtics, already 27-7 before Heinsohn went down, won 16 in a row overall.

17. A. 1949-50. The 1950 team, playing a 68-game schedule, was the last losing Celtics squad for 20 years. The 1977-78 Celtics were bad enough to cost legendary coach Tom Heinsohn his job, but Satch Sanders managed to get them to 32-50.

18. The 1950s and 1960s Celtics. But it was close. Boston won eight straight titles between 1959 and 1966 and 11 in 13 seasons between 1957 and 1969. John Wooden's legendary UCLA teams won the NCAA men's basketball title eight straight times between 1967 and 1973, and 10 in 12 years from 1964 to 1975.

19. Hondo. John Havlicek was the son of Czech immigrants, who grew up in Ohio, went to Ohio State University, and won an NCAA championship playing alongside fellow Hall of Famers Jerry Lucas and Bobby Knight.

20. B. Clippers. Following a 131-114 whipping by the Celtics at Boston Garden on April 9, 1978, the Buffalo Braves—a 1971 expansion club—relocated to San Diego and christened themselves the Clippers. They found a new location in Los Angeles in 1985. Through 2011, three of the franchise's seven playoff berths came in their stay in Buffalo.

The Larry Bird Challenge

1. A. Maurice Cheeks (West Texas A&M) was taken by the 76ers in the second round, 30 picks after Larry Bird. Mychal Thompson (first pick, Trail Blazers), Michael Ray Richardson (fourth, Knicks) and Purvis Short (fifth, Warriors) were chosen before Bird.

2. Indiana State. Despite being founded in 1896 to make them the oldest collegiate basketball team in the country, the Sycamores were forever in the shadow of Indiana University, the school Bird had originally enrolled at but had dropped out after a month. Bird led Indiana State to an undefeated season in 1978-79 before losing in the championship game against Magic Johnson and Michigan State.

3. He stayed in school. Under the NBA's "junior eligible" rule at the time, the former transfer student could go back to Indiana State for his senior year in 1978-79 and was still able to sign with the Celtics before the 1979 NBA draft.

4. False. The Celtics made the playoffs all 13 seasons of Larry Bird's career, winning 60 or more games in six of his first seven seasons and winning three NBA titles. Even with numerous injuries in the second half of his career, the Bird Celtics still never finished below .500.

5. A. 1982. Larry Bird scored 19 points, corralled 12 rebounds, and had five assists to win at the Meadowlands as Boston's Bill Fitch coached the East.

6. Bill Russell and Wilt Chamberlain. Like Larry Bird and Magic Johnson, these two great rivals were fixtures in the final between the Celtics and Lakers. Bird won his three straight MVPs starting in 1982, while Russell won his trio beginning in 1961 and Chamberlain beginning in 1965.

7. True. It was pretty select company as the NBA-heavy 1992 U.S. basketball team cruised to gold. The rest of the squad, coached by Chuck Daly: Charles Barkley, Clyde Drexler, Patrick Ewing, Magic Johnson, Michael Jordan, Christian Laettner, Karl Malone, Chris Mullin, Scottie Pippin, David Robinson and John Stockton.

Your Grandfather's Celtics

1. C. 173. The Minneapolis Lakers scored 139 points and still lost by 34. The 1959 champion Celtics scored under 100 points only four times all year, including playoffs.

2. B. Cleveland Browns. Paul Brown was always on the lookout for talent, and he brought John Havlicek to Cleveland's 1962 training camp before Hondo soon left to concentrate on basketball.

3. D. Will Greer. Greer was trying to inbound the ball with five seconds left in the seventh game of the eastern Conference finals. The steal sealed the conference title, and the Celts would go on to win the NBA crown.

4. C. Ed Macauley. He scored 1,384 points for the 1950-51 Celtics. Bob Cousy rang up 1,078 points that year but was about a month behind Macauley in the scoring department.

5. C. Doggie Julian. The former Holy Cross coach guided the Celtics from 1948-50. Red Auerbach was the right man for the job, coaching the Celtics until 1966, when he appointed Bill Russell as his successor on the bench.

6. The Basketball Association of America. A merger with the National Basketball League resulted in the creation of the National Basketball Association in 1949.

7. B. Chuck Cooper. Cooper, drafted out of West Virginia, debuted with the Celtics in 1950. Sweetwater Clifton left the Harlem Globetrotters to sign with the Knicks shortly before Cooper was drafted by Boston.

8. Tom Heinsohn, Bill Russell and K.C. Jones. All three future Hall of Famers were drafted in 1956. Heinsohn and Jones by the Celtics. The highly sought-after Russell was taken with

the first pick by the St. Louis Hawks and traded to the Celtics for All-Star Ed Macauley and Cliff Hagen, who had been serving in the military.

9. C. 1957. The Celtics had lost in the playoffs six straight years without reaching the finals before finally—and forever—changing the team's fortunes in '57.

10. C. The St. Louis Hawks. The Hawks and Celtics had pulled off a blockbuster trade before the season and would meet again in the finals the following year. The Celtics reached the finals by beating the Syracuse Nationals.

11. B. He was ejected from a major league game without ever playing in one, getting thumbed along with the entire Dodgers bench in a game on September 27, 1951. As a September call-up he witnessed Brooklyn's once massive National League lead dwindle to nothing as the Giants, with a fiendish sign-stealing scheme, stole the pennant.

12. A. Gene Conley. Signed by both the Boston Braves and Boston Celtics, he won a World Series ring in 1957, after the Braves moved to Milwaukee. A four-time All-Star pitcher, he was a three-time world champion as a backup center for the Celtics.

13. Nine. Red Auerbach won nine titles between 1950-66, including eight in a row to finish that run.

14. C. 90. Red Auerbach won 90 out of 148 postseason games, the most in Celtics history.

15. D. Ed Macauley. He spent six seasons with the Celtics in the 1950s, averaging 18.9 points per game. He was inducted into the Hall of Fame in 1960. Hall of Famers to follow included Walter Brown in 1965, Red Auerbach in 1968, and Bob Cousy in 1970.

16. False. Bob Cousy had the same average of 18.5 points per game in the regular season and in the playoffs. Talk about consistent.

17. C. Curt Gowdy. Johnny Most, a protégé of New York announcing legend Marty Glickman, took over for Gowdy in 1953. Most remained in the Celtics booth until 1990. His 1965 "Havlicek stole the ball" call is arguably the most famous sound bite in Celtics history.

18. False. Red Auerbach played exactly one game in the pros, for Harrisburg of the American Basketball League in 1942-43,

scoring one career point. He had far more success directing a bench than sitting on it.

19. A. Boston College. Bob Cousy coached the Eagles to a 114-38 record in six seasons. His 1966-67 Eagles went 21-3 and reached the Elite Eight in the NCAAs, and the 1968-69 squad went 24-4 and reached the NIT final before falling. Cousy did not have as much success coaching in the NBA.

20. False. The Celtics spurned the Holy Cross All-American when he was available in the 1950 draft. Bob Cousy was taken by the Tri-Cities (now Atlanta) Hawks and sent to the Chicago Stags. That club folded, and Cousy went to Boston in the NBA dispersal draft of Stags players. The Celts still didn't want him but fate handed them him, anyway.

The Bill Russell Challenge

1. D. San Francisco. The Dons, the only team to offer Bill Russell a scholarship, won the NCAA title in 1955 and 1956. USF was the first team to win a title with three African American starters: Russell, Jones and Hal Perry. Perry briefly played for the Harlem Globetrotters before becoming a lawyer.

2. He was leading the U.S. Olympic team to a gold medal at the 1956 Olympic Games in Melbourne. Bill Russell arrived to find a 13-3 team, but he fit in nicely and helped Boston claim its first championship.

3. C. 51. Bill Russell was the first to break the 50-rebound barrier against the Philadelphia Warriors in 1959-60. Nemesis Wilt Chamberlain of the Warriors broke Russell's mark against the Celtics with 55 the following year. Russell's 32 rebounds in a half remains a record, and he is also second to Wilt in career rebounds (21,620).

4. D. 114. That is a .597 winning percentage with Russell owning an 85-57 advantage when facing Chamberlain teams and a 29-20 edge in postseason competition, including a 4-0 mark in Game 7 situations.

5. C. *Saturday Night Live.* Bill Russell hosted the show in 1979, playing a coach of an all-white team in "The Black Shadow" and being serenaded in Greenland by lounge singer Bill Murray. The next basketball player to host *SNL* was Michael Jordan in 1991.

6. False. Bill Russell took over for Red Auerbach in 1966-67 and won two championships in three years. Dave Cowens was

player-coach for the Celtics in 1978-79. Hall of Fame Celtics Bob Cousy and Ed Macauley were player-coaches but with other teams.

7. 11. A remarkable total for a remarkable player who changed the game.

Celtics in the Rafters

1. B. Walter Brown. The second generation of his family to run the Boston Garden, he was the original owner of the Celtics and was also instrumental in Boston hockey.

2. Red Auerbach. He came in four seasons after the team started, but he forged the Celtics with his own two hands.

3. 00. The Celtics retired the number in 1998, a year after Robert Parish retired and five years before he got the inevitable call to the Basketball Hall of Fame.

4. C. K.C. Jones. He was the first and last to don number 25, wearing it proudly from 1959 to 1967 before starting another great career as coach of the Celtics and adding yet more trophies to the franchise's haul.

5. It's not a slur snuck up there by an anti-Celtics faction, it stands for "Microphone." That distinction—and distinctive voice—belongs to none other than Johnny Most, legendary Celtics play-by-play man (1953-1990).

6. Don Nelson. Nelson averaged 10 points per game and led the NBA in field goal percentage in 1974-75 at .539. He retired a year later and debuted as a head coach with the Milwaukee Bucks in 1976-77. He was still coaching more than three decades later.

7. A-15, B-22, C-31, D-21

8. 21. That's right 21 numbers are retired by the Celtics. It's no wonder the 2011 team broke out first-time numbers 77, 86, and 88!

The Colleges

Boston College

1. Who caught Doug Flutie's miraculous 48-yard touchdown pass on the final play to beat the University of Miami on November 23, 1984?

2. The 1942 Eagles football team was ranked number one before they were upset by Holy Cross, 55-12. Because of the drubbing, BC cancelled a party on a night when what popular Boston night club caught fire and killed hundreds of people?

3. What is the nickname of the Boston College mascot?

4. What school did the Eagles beat for the 2010 NCAA hockey title?
   A. Minnesota
   B. North Dakota
   C. Notre Dame
   D. Wisconsin

5. True or false? Boston College men's basketball has never reached the Final Four.

6. Which year did Boston College leave the Big East for the ACC?
   A. 2003
   B. 2005
   C. 2007
   D. 2009

7. What conference does Boston College compete in for hockey?

8. "The Commonwealth Classic" is the nickname for basketball games between Boston College and what other school?

9. In the 2008 NFL draft the Atlanta Falcons made quarterback Matt Ryan the highest-chosen BC player in history. What overall selection in the draft did the Falcons use on Matty Ice?
   A. First
   B. Third
   C. Fifth
   D. Seventh

10. The first captain of the Boston College football team was later elected to the U.S. House of Representatives. Who was he?

A. James Carlin

B. Joseph Drum

C. Joseph F. O'Connell

D. Tip O'Neill

11. How many touchdowns did Doug Flutie pass for during his four years at Boston College?

A. 47

B. 57

C. 67

D. 77

12. Which year did Doug Flutie win the Heisman Trophy?

A. 1982

B. 1984

C. 1986

D. 1988

13. How many passes did Darren Flutie catch from older brother Doug at BC?

A. 0

B. 9

C. 28

D. 45

14. True or false? Darren Flutie was inducted into the Canadian Football Hall of Fame before his older brother Doug.

15. When Doug Flutie took Boston College to a bowl game in 1982, how long had it been since their last appearance in the post season?

    A. 10 years

    B. 20 years

    C. 30 years

    D. 40 years

16. Boston College was an independent in football for 100 seasons. What year did BC join the Big East in football?

    A. 1981

    B. 1986

    C. 1991

    D. 1996

17. John Loughery, a Boston College quarterback from 1979-82, was uncle to which future BC quarterback?

    A. Doug Flutie

    B. Glenn Foley

    C. Matt Hasselback

    D. Matt Ryan

18. The winner of the 1985 Outland Trophy was a BC defensive lineman named...

    A. Anthony Costanzo

    B. Ryan Poles

    C. George Ruth

    D. Mike Ruth

19. Boston College put together a bowl winning streak at the start of the 21st century that covered how many consecutive years?

A. 4

B. 6

C. 8

D. 10

20. What kind of person did legendary Eagles hockey coach Snooks Kelly refuse to have play for him at Boston College?

A. Canadians

B. Husbands

C. Protestants

D. Smokers

21. Boston College can lay claim to the all-time American-born point scorer in NHL history. Who was he?

22. What are the most goals put in the net in a game by Boston College?

A. 12

B. 16

C. 20

D. 24

23. This Boston College defenseman was the school's first hockey All-American and was later the first quarterback in Patriots history. Who was he?

    A. Jim Logue

    B. Tim Sheehy

    C. Butch Songin

    D. Luke Urban

24. Goalie Tim Ready set a Boston College record for most saves in a game. How many Princeton shots did he stop on February 11, 1936?

    A. 60

    B. 71

    C. 82

    D. 93

25. Boston College and Princeton were asked to represent the U.S. against Canadian schools in the first college hockey games ever played at which arena in 1925?

    A. Boston Garden

    B. Madison Square Garden

    C. Maple Leaf Gardens

    D. Montreal Forum

26. Who scored the overtime goal in 2001 to win Boston College's first national championship in hockey in 52 years?

    A. Scott Clemmensen

    B. Chuck Kobasew

    C. Krys Kolanos

    D. Rob Scuderi

27. Who was the first Boston College skater to win the Hobey Baker Award as the nation's top collegiate hockey player?

A. David Emma

B. Craig Janney

C. Brian Leetch

D. Tim Sweeney

28. Boston College coaching legend John "Snooks" Kelley was the first college hockey coach to reach 500 wins. Which rival did Snooks get his landmark 500th win against?

A. Boston University

B. Dartmouth

C. Harvard

D. Notre Dame

29. On the remarkable 1987 BC team that included six future NHL players, who was named team MVP as a freshman?

30. Which Boston College men's basketball star was twice named Big East Player of the Year?

A. Michael Adams

B. Troy Bell

C. Bill Curley

D. Jared Dudley

Answers on pages 124-127

The Holy War

1. Where was the first football game played in the "Holy War" between Boston College and Notre Dame?

   A. Alumni Stadium

   B. Fenway Park

   C. The Liberty Bowl

   D. Foxboro Stadium

2. True or false? The first win on the football field by Boston College over Notre Dame knocked the Irish out of the number-one ranking in the country.

3. Whose field goal won the legendary 1993 game for Boston College against Notre Dame?

4. What is the longest football winning streak by Boston College against Notre Dame in the "Holy War"?

   A. 2

   B. 4

   C. 6

   D. 8

5. What legendary football coach spent time at both Boston College and Notre Dame?

6. The Snooks Kelley-Lefty Smith Trophy is given to the winner of the Boston College-Notre Dame game in which sport?

7. Boston College beat Notre Dame for the NCAA men's hockey championship in what year?
   A. 1969
   B. 1981
   C. 1997
   D. 2008

8. Which rivalry between Boston College-Notre Dame is older: football or hockey?

Answers on page 127

Boston University

1. Boston College and Boston University played football 32 times between 1893 and 1962. How many times did the Terriers win?

   A. 4

   B. 8

   C. 12

   D. 16

2. Which of the following is *not* a popular nickname for the Boston College-Boston University rivalry?

   A. Battle of Commonwealth Ave.

   B. Bird-Dog Battle

   C. B-Line Rivalry

   D. Green Line Rivalry

3. Who won the first hockey game played between Boston University and Boston College in 1918?

4. What is the name of the Boston University mascot?

5. Boston University hockey played on the smallest ice surface in NCAA Division I during its time at what arena from 1971-2005?

6. Hockey jersey number 24 was retired for which former BU player?

7. The "Miracle on Ice" goalie for the 1980 Winter Games at Lake Placid was from Boston University. Name him.

8. Name the BU player who last controlled the puck as Al Michaels did his famous countdown of the final seconds of the 1980 Winter Games "Miracle on Ice" against the USSR in Lake Placid.

9. What BU player served as captain for the 1980 Winter Games "Miracle on Ice" team?

10. This former BU defenseman was drafted by both the NHL and WHA in 1977, but he stayed at Boston University, was 1978 tournament MVP for NCAA champion Terriers, and played for the 1980 "Miracle on Ice" U.S. hockey team. Who was he?

11. How many years did Boston University field a football team before it was discontinued in 1997?
    A. 31
    B. 51
    C. 71
    D. 91

12. BU alum Bill Brooks had 1,100 yards receiving and eight touchdowns as a rookie in 1986 for which NFL team?

    A. Baltimore Colts

    B. Baltimore Ravens

    C. Indianapolis Colts

    D. New England Patriots

13. This BU alum played 12 years in the NFL, mostly as a wide receiver for the Cleveland Browns. In the 1980s he served as a broadcaster for both the Cleveland Indians and AFC football on NBC. Can you name him?

14. The Boston University basketball and hockey teams play in an arena named after the school's first football All-American. Who was this beloved legend from Lynn who played first base for the Red Sox and was known as "The Golden Greek"?

15. This baseball Hall of Famer played at BU, was a two-time AL MVP, was catcher for the Philadelphia A's three straight pennant winners in 1929-31, and served as player-manager for the Tigers for two more pennants. Who was he?

16. True or false? Boston University has the largest enrollment of any private school in the country without a football team.

17. This Little League World Series-winning pitcher was inducted into the Boston University Hall of Fame for ice hockey. Name him.

18. Boston University had the second-longest streak in women's college soccer history with a shutout streak of how many games?
    A. 7
    B. 10
    C. 13
    D. 16

19. Which team did Boston University defeat for the NCAA hockey title in 2009?
    A. Clarkson
    B. Miami
    C. Michigan
    D. North Dakota State

20. Who scored the overtime goal that gave Boston University the 2009 NCAA men's ice hockey title?

Answers on pages 128-129

Harvard

1. The Ivy League represents eight schools in seven states. Name all eight Ivy League schools and their home states.

2. In a battle of Harvard alums, Steve Adams (class of 1999) was defending Dominic Moore (class of 2003) when Moore's no-look pass resulted in the only goal in Game 7 to clinch a first-round series victory in the 2011 NHL playoffs. Which team did Moore help reach the next round?
    A. Boston Bruins
    B. New York Rangers
    C. Pittsburgh Penguins
    D. Tampa Bay Lightning

3. Through 2011, who was the only Harvard alum in NFL history to be named first-team All-Pro?
    A. John Dockery
    B. Ryan Fitzpatrick
    C. Pat McInally
    D. Joe Pellegrini

4. Which Harvard alum has played in the most Pro Bowls?
    A. Matt Birk
    B. Desmond Bryant
    C. Ryan Fitzgerald
    D. Pat McInally

5. The 2006 season marked the first time in 82 years that an NFL team had two Harvard alums on a roster at the same time. What team put two former Crimson players on the roster?

A. Arizona Cardinals

B. New England Patriots

C. San Francisco 49ers

D. St. Louis Rams

6. True or false? No one has ever played a down for the Patriots after being drafted by the team out of Harvard.

7. Who was the first person to play for both Harvard and the Boston Celtics?

A. Joe Carrabino

B. Wyndol Gray

C. Saul Mariaschin

D. Ed Smith

8. Harvard beat a nationally ranked team in men's basketball for the first time in school history on January 9, 2009. Which team did the Crimson beat?

A. Boston College

B. Kansas

C. North Carolina

D. Syracuse

9. Before making the NCAA tournament in 2012, Harvard had played in the tournament just once in 110 years. What year was it?

   A. 1936

   B. 1946

   C. 1956

   D. 1966

10. True or false? The Harvard men's basketball team played in the National Invitational Tournament for the first time in school history in 2011.

11. Against whom did Harvard share its first-ever Ivy League men's basketball title in 2011?

12. Harvard played its first intercollegiate football game against an American opponent on June 4, 1875. Who was it against?

    A. Boston College

    B. Princeton

    C. Tufts

    D. Yale

13. True or false? Harvard Stadium is the oldest stadium in football.

14. Lights were installed at Harvard Stadium in 2007. Who was their first nocturnal opponent?

    A. Brown

    B. Columbia

    C. Dartmouth

    D. Yale

15. Brutality in football at the turn of the 20th century threatened to end the sport. Calls to widen the field would have made Harvard's new concrete stadium obsolete. Who developed the forward pass, enabling the field to remain the same size, thus saving Harvard Stadium?

    A. Walter Camp

    B. John Heisman

    C. Knute Rockne

    D. Teddy Roosevelt

16. Harvard was credited with eight college football national championships. What year was the Crimson's last one?

    A. 1890

    B. 1898

    C. 1910

    D. 1919

17. The 1919 Crimson scored 222 points and allowed only 13 points during the calendar year. Which team scored 10 of those points to tie Harvard?

    A. Colby

    B. Oregon

    C. Princeton

    D. Yale

18. The Harvard women's ice hockey team won the 1999 NCAA championship with a 6-5 win over New Hampshire in the final. Harvard wrapped up the trophy with how many consecutive wins?

A. 24

B. 27

C. 30

D. 33

19. Harvard is part of the oldest college hockey rivalry with which school?

A. Boston College

B. Boston University

C. Brown

D. Yale

20. The first college racing shell was raced by Harvard in what year?

A. 1849

B. 1859

C. 1869

D. 1879

21. How many miles is the Harvard-Yale regatta?

22. Six months after Jackie Robinson debuted in the major leagues, Harvard's star tackle Chester Pierce became the first African American to play against a white college in the South on October 11, 1947. Which Southern school did the Crimson visit?

A. Alabama

B. Mississippi

C. North Carolina

D. Virginia

23. Who won the Ivy League Men's Basketball Player of the Year Award for Harvard in 2011?

24. Which three-time All-American and future Women's Professional League Soccer midfielder missed the 1997 season at Harvard to donate bone marrow and be with her brother in his fight against leukemia?

A. Brandi Chastain

B. Mia Hamm

C. Emily Stauffer

D. Sara Whalen

25. The 1998 Harvard women's basketball team became the first 16 seed to beat a 1 seed in NCAA basketball tournament history. Which perennial power did Harvard stun?

A. Connecticut

B. Notre Dame

C. Stanford

D. Tennessee

26. Through 2011, who was the last Harvard man to be named a Walter Camp All-American?
    A. Matt Birk
    B. Ryan Fitzpatrick
    C. Pat McInally
    D. Endicott Peabody

27. Harvard alum Emily Cross won a silver medal in the Beijing Olympics in which sport?
    A. Equestrian
    B. Fencing
    C. Javelin
    D. Team Handball

28. Eddie Grant, the longest tenured Harvard alum in the major leagues, had a plaque in his memory erected in deep center field at which former New York ballpark?
    A. Ebbets Field
    B. Polo Grounds
    C. Shea Stadium
    D. Yankee Stadium

29. In the 1990 NCAA women's lacrosse championship, Harvard came from four goals down to upset which perennial lax power?
    A. Duke
    B. Johns Hopkins
    C. Maryland
    D. Princeton

30. Sister and brother Jordanna and Jeremy Fraiberg both won national championships on the same day in 1992 in which sport?

A. Fencing

B. Squash

C. Swimming

D. Tennis

Answers on pages 129-133

'The Game'

1. Long known as simply "The Game," Harvard and Yale have been playing each other in football since which year?

   A. 1870

   B. 1875

   C. 1880

   D. 1885

2. Harvard beat Yale in the final game of 2001 to record the Crimson's first unbeaten, untied season since what year?

   A. 1913

   B. 1923

   C. 1933

   D. 1943

3. In the Ivy League's first triple-overtime game, in 2005, the go-ahead touchdown was scored by the Ivy League's all-time leading scorer and rusher. Who was he?

   A. Clifton Dawson

   B. Teddy DeMars

   C. Hamilton Fish

   D. Collie Winters

4. The 1987 Harvard football team clinched an Ivy League title and an undefeated season with a thrilling 14-10 win at the Yale Bowl. Which other Harvard school also clinched the Ivy title the same frigid day in New Haven?

A. Cross country

B. Field hockey

C. Men's soccer

D. Women's soccer

5. Harvard's fabled 1968 "win" over Yale was actually a tie, but it preserved Harvard's first undefeated season since 1920. The furious Crimson rally tied the score at what prime number?

A. 17

B. 29

C. 37

D. 43

6. What future Oscar-winning actor's final game was at offensive tackle in one of the most famous editions of "The Game" in 1968?

7. Which school won the 100th version of "The Game" in 1983?

Answers on page 133

Northeastern

1. Northeastern men's basketball played its first game in 1920 against which New England school?

   A. Boston College

   B. Harvard

   C. Harvard Law

   D. Maine

2. Northeastern made the NCAA men's basketball tournament for the first time in which year?

   A. 1971

   B. 1976

   C. 1981

   D. 1986

3. Which team did Northeastern beat in its first NCAA men's basketball tournament game?

   A. Fresno State

   B. Howard

   C. Indiana

   D. Utah

4. In its first 34 years of men's basketball, Northeastern played its home games at which arena?

   A. Boston Garden

   B. Boston YMCA

   C. Cabot Center

   D. Matthews Arena

5. True or false? Dick Dukeshire has the most wins of any coach in Northeastern men's basketball history.

6. In the seven years that Jim Calhoun coached Northeastern in the America East tournament, how many times did the Huskies earn an NCAA tournament trip?

7. Who was the first Northeastern basketball player to play in the NBA?
   A. Jose Barea
   B. Harry Barnes
   C. Reggie Lewis
   D. Perry Moss

8. Who is the highest-scoring player in Northeastern men's basketball history?
   A. Jose Barea
   B. Pete Harris
   C. Matt Janning
   D. Reggie Lewis

9. The Northeastern women's basketball team played its first game in which year?
   A. 1946
   B. 1956
   C. 1966
   D. 1976

10. The Northeastern women's basketball team reached 100 points for the first time in school history in 2010. Against which team did they hit the century mark?

    A. Drexel

    B. George Mason

    C. Hofstra

    D. Old Dominion

11. True or false? Jim Calhoun was inducted into the Northeaster Hall of Fame while he was still coaching at the school.

12. Northeastern had its most successful year in 2002-03 when it won a school record number of titles. Out of 14 sports, how many conference titles did NU win?

13. What year did Northeastern play its final football game after 74 years of existence as a program?

    A. 1997

    B. 2002

    C. 2009

    D. 2011

14. Which year did Northeastern make its lone College World Series appearance?

    A. 1946

    B. 1956

    C. 1966

    D. 1976

15. In 2011 Northeastern had the most players chosen in the major league baseball draft than in any year in school history. How many Huskies were picked by big league organizations?

16. What major league All-Star's brother played at Northeastern and was drafted by two different major league clubs?
    A. Mike Glavine
    B. Bill O'Leary
    C. Mike Maguire
    D. Omar Pena

17. True or false? Former American League home run champion Carlos Pena is the all-time home-run leader at Northeastern.

18. Northeastern's Dan Ross set a Super Bowl record with 11 catches for which team?
    A. Cincinnati Bengals
    B. Denver Broncos
    C. San Francisco 49ers
    D. Washington Redskins

19. NFL tight end Dan Ross had his number retired at Northeastern. What number was it?
    A. 1
    B. 10
    C. 82
    D. 84

20. Through 2011, Northeastern men's and women's track teams had combined for 24 New England titles since 1969, but the Huskies had won just one individual NCAA championship. It was by Boris Djerassi in which event?

A. Discus

B. Hammer throw

C. Shot put

D. Weight lifting

Answers on pages 134-136

Beanpot Challenge

1. Name the four schools involved annually in the Beanpot Hockey Tournament.

2. Who won the first Beanpot men's hockey title, in 1952?

3. What former Bruin played on the first Bruins Stanley Cup champion, coached the B's to another Cup, and was the winning coach in the first Beanpot tournament. Who was he?

   A. Dit Clapper

   B. Eddie Shore

   C. Tiny Thompson

   D. Cooney Weiland

4. Which school was the last of the four to win a Beanpot men's hockey title?

5. This former Olympian holds the Beanpot record for most goals in a tournament, and he also worked the Beanpot as an official, a coach, and an athletic director. Who is this Boston hockey institution?

   A. Bill Cleary

   B. Ted Drury

   C. Mike Eruzione

   D. Dave Silk

6. Which school has won the most Beanpot men's hockey titles?

7. What year did the Beanpot Women's Hockey Tournament begin?
   A. 1979
   B. 1984
   C. 1989
   D. 1994

8. When Boston University gave up baseball, which college took its place in the annual Beanpot Baseball Tournament in 1996?

Answers on page 136

College Knowledge

1. This former governor of Massachusetts played football at Bentley and Boston Colleges and then played in the NFL before going into politics. Who was he?

   A. Mike Dukakis

   B. Ed King

   C. Deval Patrick

   D. Bill Weld

2. Late Yankees owner George Steinbrenner's father was a world-class hurdler at which area college in the 1920s?

   A. Boston University

   B. Harvard

   C. Holy Cross

   D. Massachusetts Institute of Technology

3. Which college hosted the Patriots for their first game in the American Football League in 1960?

   A. Boston College

   B. Boston University

   C. Harvard

   D. Northeastern

4. Which college hosted the Patriots for their final season in the American Football League in 1969?

   A. Boston College

   B. Boston University

   C. Harvard

   D. Northeastern

5. Which college hosted the Patriots for their first year in the National Football League in 1970?

   A. Boston College

   B. Boston University

   C. Harvard

   D. Northeastern

6. Emerson College's Jim Peckham served as head coach for the U.S. in which Olympic sport in the 1976 Montreal Games?

   A. Badminton

   B. Greco-Roman Wrestling

   C. Gymnastics

   D. Sailing

7. To give the school the required same number of men's and women's sports in 2011, Lesley University in Cambridge added which sport?

   A. Baseball

   B. Cross-Country

   C. Softball

   D. Tennis

8. Tufts University's athletic teams have a nickname that derives from a gift from famed promoter and circus owner P.T. Barnum in the 1880s. What is the nickname?

9. Which year did Tufts go to the NCAA men's basketball tournament?

   A. 1940

   B. 1945

   C. 1950

   D. 1955

10. Mackenzy Bernadeau, a guard for the Carolina Panthers, became the first-ever NFL player drafted out of his hometown college in Waltham, Massachusetts. What school was it?

11. Which local college did the Red Sox use as a spring training facility in 1943 due to travel restrictions in World War II?

    A. Babson College

    B. Emerson College

    C. Harvard College

    D. Tufts University

12. Which Division III college hosts athletic events at Roberto Clemente Field, less than a mile from Fenway Park?

    A. Emerson

    B. Emmanuel

    C. Simmons

    D. Wheelock

13. What is the nickname for Brandeis College athletic teams?

    A. Eagles

    B. Ephs

    C. Falcons

    D. Judges

14. Name one of the three former Celtics who have coached men's basketball at Brandeis College in Waltham?

15. What is the nickname for UMass-Boston athletics teams?

    A. Beacons

    B. Deacons

    C. Minutemen

    D. Sharks

16. UMass-Boston hosts the second-oldest college annual hockey tournament in the country. What is this tournament called?

17. Thomas Pelham Curtis won the 110 meter hurdles in the first modern Olympics in 1896 as a student at which Boston school?

    A. Harvard

    B. Emerson

    C. Massachusetts Institute of Technology

    D. Tufts

18. In 1972 Alan Dopfel threw MIT's first no-hitter and led the country in strikeouts, becoming the first Engineer drafted by a major league team. Which team picked him that year in the third round?

A. Boston Red Sox

B. California Angels

C. Montreal Expos

D. New York Yankees

19. Who was drafted out of UMass-Lowell in the first round of the 2000 NHL draft?

A. Kevin Charboneau

B. Dana Demole

C. Ron Hainsey

D. Dwayne Roloson

20. Jon Norris, a seven-time Pro Bowl center, was drafted by the Patriots out of which area school in 1964?

A. Curry College

B. Fitchburg State

C. Holy Cross

D. MIT

Answers on pages 136-138

Boston College

1. Gerard Phelan. His catch on national TV the day after Thanksgiving gave BC a stunning 47-45 win in Miami and built on the already growing mystique of the Flutie legend.

2. The Cocoanut Grove. The former speakeasy caught fire on the night of November 28, 1942. It was the most deadly nightclub fire ever on the East Coast, taking the lives of 492 people.

3. Baldwin. It comes from "Bald" for the bald eagle and "win" for what BC teams all hope to do.

4. D. Wisconsin. BC blanked the Badgers, 5-0, for the 2010 NCAA hockey championship, their fourth title. The Eagles reached the Frozen Four for the 23rd time in 2012.

5. True. Through 2012, they have come agonizingly close, losing the regional final in 1967 (to North Carolina), 1982 (to Houston) and 1994 (Florida).

6. B. 2005. BC was a founding member of the Big East but officially joined the Atlantic Coast Conference on July 1, 2005.

7. Hockey East. The Atlantic Coast Conference doesn't do hockey at a Division I level.

8. UMass Amherst. Massachusetts and BC played for the first time in men's basketball in 1905 and have been playing regularly since 1995, with BC winning 26 of the first 45 installments.

9. B. The third overall pick. The Falcons took Matt Ryan after the Dolphins took tackle Jake Long and the Rams took defensive tackle Chris Long (no relation).

10. C. Joseph F. O'Connell. Joseph Drum and O'Connell petitioned BC president Edward Ignatius Devitt to found a varsity football team in 1892. O'Connell, a future U.S. Congressman,

was captain. Drum served as the unpaid head coach. The running back from that first BC team, James Carlin, later served as president of rival Holy Cross.

11. C. 67. Flutie threw 67 TD passes, including 27 in his Heisman Trophy season.

12. B. 1984. Doug Flutie won the Heisman Trophy over Keith Byars of Ohio State, Robbie Bosco of BYU, Bernie Kosar of Miami and TCU's Kenneth Davis.

13. B. 9. Darren Flutie was a freshman as big brother on campus Doug was taking college football by storm in 1984. They had another brief tenure at BC in 1991—for British Columbia in the Canadian Football League.

14. True. Darren, a former BC receiver who had 1,000 yards receiving nine times in the CFL, was inducted in 2007. Doug, who quarterbacked three fewer seasons in Canada but was MVP of three Grey Cups, was inducted a year later.

15. D. 40 years. The Eagles had last played in the 1942 Orange Bowl, losing to Alabama, before Flutie and Co. led BC to the 1982 Tangerine Bowl, losing to Auburn.

16. C. 1991. BC first started playing football in 1892.

17. D. Matt Ryan. John Loughery was the starting quarterback at BC when Doug Flutie arrived in 1981 and took the job. His nephew manned the position from 2004-07.

18. D. Mike Ruth. Ruth was taken in the second round in 1986 by the Patriots and spent two years with the team. (George Herman "Babe" Ruth excelled in another sport.)

19. C. 8. Between 2000 and 2007 BC won eight straight bowl games over eight different schools: Arizona State, Georgia, Toledo, Colorado State, North Carolina, Boise State, Michigan State and Navy.

20. A. Canadians. He only recruited American kids. The coach put it this way in *Sports Illustrated* in 1968: "I want to play the kid that used to make sodas down at the drugstore and who caddies during the summer. His kind has proved to me it can play hockey with the best."

21. Joe Mullen. He played at BC from 1975-79, and he was the first American to reach the 500-goal plateau and win three Stanley Cups in a four-year span: Calgary in 1989 and Pittsburgh in 1991 and 1992.

22. D. 24. On December 27, 1939, Cornell suffered a fate worse than being forced to consume a rancid fruitcake in a 24-1 shelling by BC. The Eagles set numerous records, including six goals in a game (by John Pryor) and 11 points apiece (by Pryor and Ray Chaisson).

23. C. Butch Songin. He was a member of the 1949 national champion Eagles and recorded 77 points (33 goals and 44 assists) in 63 games. As BC's QB he threw for 30 TDs. Songin, who had last played in the Canadian Football League in 1954, appeared in every Patriots game in 1961 and 1962, recording the lowest interception percentage both years in the pass-happy AFL.

24. C. 82. Tim Ready was ready all right, stopping 63 Princeton shots in regulation and another 19 in overtime.

25. B. Madison Square Garden. BC won both games against the Canadian schools, beating the Royal Military Academy, 7-6, and the University of Montreal, 4-2, on December 28 and 29, 1925.

26. C. Krys Kolanos. His goal not only gave BC its first championship in any sport since 1949, he ended three straight years of losing in the NCAA final. What's more, North Dakota scored twice against goalie Scott Clemmensen in the last 3:42 to force overtime before Kolanos came through at 4:43 of OT to end the Frozen Four in Albany.

27. A. David Emma. BC's career scoring leader (239 points), he won the 1991 Baker Award with 81 points in 39 games. The right wing from Rhode Island spent time in Europe and the NHL, including a few games as a Boston Bruin. His number 16 was the first number retired for a BC hockey player.

28. A. Boston University. BC beat BU by a score of 7-2 for Snooks Kelley's 500th win on February 23, 1972. It was the next-to-last win of his remarkable 36-year career that saw him go 501-243-15, including the 1949 title over Dartmouth, the first national hockey title by an Eastern school.

29. Brian Leetch. A future Hockey Hall of Famer and the son of BC All-American Jack Leetch, he beat out teammates—and future NHL players—Greg Brown, Craig Janney, Ken Hodge, Kevin Stevens and Tim Sweeney. The freshman also won the Walter Brown Award, given annually to the top American-born player in New England.

30. B. Troy Bell. He won Big East Player of the Year as a sopho-

more in 2001 and again as a senior in 2003. With 2,632 career points, he is the school's all-time leading scorer. Jared Dudley was ACC Player of the Year in 2007, after BC's exodus from the Big East.

The Holy War

1. D. Foxboro Stadium. The teams met for the first time on the gridiron in 1975, with Notre Dame winning, 17-3. They met again eight years later at the Liberty Bowl, a narrow 19-18 Irish win. The teams have played on an almost annual basis since 1992.

2. True. Notre Dame was number one, and the Eagles were number 17 when they met in South Bend on November 20, 1993.

3. David Gordon. The left-footed kicker's 41-yarder with five seconds left appeared to be going right, but it changed trajectory and split the uprights for a 41-39 win to knock the Irish from the unbeaten ranks. Florida State ended up number one and Notre Dame number two, although the Irish had beaten the Seminoles during the season. BC was 12th.

4. C. 6. With Notre Dame owning a 9-3 edge in the series in 2001, BC reeled off six straight victories against the Irish: three in Chestnut Hill and three in South Bend.

5. Frank Leahy. A trophy in his name is given to the winner of each BC-ND game (plus the Ireland Trophy). A Notre Dame grad, Leahy's first head coaching job was at Boston College. His Eagles went 20-2 in 1939-40, capped off with a Sugar Bowl victory. He returned to Notre Dame and coached four national champions.

6. Hockey. It is named for the legendary coaches of the two schools: Snooks Kelley (BC) and Lefty Smith (ND).

7. D. 2008. Leading scorer Nathan Gerbe came through with the first two goals of the game and added two assists. John Muse made it stand up for a 4-1 BC victory over the Irish to culminate the Frozen Four in Denver.

8. Hockey. The first meeting on the ice was December 20, 1969, with Boston College winning 7-3 at home. Nine days later BC won in South Bend, 7-4. By the 1975 inaugural football game between the schools, BC-ND hockey was an annual rite.

Boston University

1. A. 4. Boston University had a 4-27-1 mark in football against Boston College, with the last win in 1959.

2. B. Bird-Dog Battle. Though accurate in an animal sense, the rivalry between the Eagles and Terriers has generally gone by other handles. *The Battle of Commonwealth Ave.* was the name of a 2009 documentary by Rival Films.

3. Boston College. But 1918 was BU's first year playing hockey. By 1934 the Terriers controlled the rivalry and had an 11-game unbeaten streak against BC. Despite gains by BC since 2010, BU still holds a series edge.

4. Rhett the Terrier. Ruff!

5. Walter Brown Arena. Brown was the original owner of the Celtics and former president of the Bruins. The Walter Brown Award is annually given to the best American-born player in New England.

6. Travis Roy. In 1995, just 11 seconds into his first college shift, Roy slid head first into the boards when a North Dakota player avoided his check. He was left a quadriplegic. He graduated from the BU College of Communications, wrote a book, and set up a foundation to help spinal cord research.

7. Jim Craig. The hero of the Games, he played in just 30 NHL games after the Olympics.

8. Dave Silk. As Al Michaels called it—on tape delay!—on ABC: "Eleven seconds, you've got ten seconds, the countdown going on right now! Morrow, up to Silk. Five seconds left in the game. Do you believe in miracles?...YES!"

9. Mike Eruzione. He did not play high-level hockey after the Olympics, saying he had accomplished all of his goals in the game. Hard to argue with him.

10. Jack O'Callahan. He was two-time team captain at BU and was injured for part of the 1980 Olympics, but he was back for the "Miracle on Ice" game against the USSR.

11. D. 91 years. BU sent 38 players to the NFL.

12. C. Indianapolis Colts. Bill Brooks was in the top 10 in yards and touchdowns in the NFL as a rookie for the Colts. The fourth-round pick out of BU also returned punts.

13. Reggie Rucker. He played in the NFL from 1970-81, was an Indians announcer from 1982-84, and was with NBC from 1983-88. Through 2011 he still covered the Browns on Cleveland television, and he even began a reconciliation between the team and all-time great Jim Brown.

14. Harry Agganis. In 1951 he was winner of the Bulger Lowe Award as New England's outstanding football player. He turned down numerous offers to go pro in football and instead signed with the Red Sox. He died of a pulmonary embolism at age 26 in 1955 in his second season with the Sox.

15. Mickey Cochrane. The Bridgewater native was one of the all-time great backstops, batting .320 for his career and managing the Tigers to their first world championship in 1935—scoring the deciding run in walkoff fashion to clinch the World Series over the Cubs.

16. False. New York University, which dropped football in the 1960s, has some 11,000 more students than BU. At last count, Boston University's 30,000-plus students placed fourth in private school enrollment behind NYU, USC and BYU.

17. Chris Drury. He pitched Trumbull, Connecticut, to the Little League World Series title in 1989, the same year he also led his pee wee hockey team to the national championship. The Hobey Baker Award winner while at BU, Drury spent 18 seasons in the NHL and also represented his country in two Olympics.

18. C. 13. BU kept opponents off the scoreboard for 13 straight games and 1,260 minutes, 38 seconds. That's 21 scoreless hours. Not surprisingly, freshman goalie Kelli King was America East Rookie of the Year.

19. B. Miami… of Ohio, that is. BU pulled out a 4-3 overtime victory in the 2009 Frozen Four final in Washington to capture the school's fifth championship.

20. Colby Cohen. The sophomore defenseman scored the championship winner on a pass from Kevin Shattenkirk. Cohen earned the 2009 Frozen Four Most Outstanding Player.

Harvard

1. Brown (Rhode Island), Columbia and Cornell (New York), Dartmouth (New Hampshire), Harvard (Massachusetts), Princeton (New Jersey), University of Pennsylvania (don't

need to be an Ivy Leaguer to guess the state here) and Yale (Connecticut).

2. D. Tampa Bay Lightning. Dominic Moore's assist helped the Lightning rally from a three games-to-one deficit against Steve Adams' Pittsburgh Penguins in the first round of the 2011 playoffs.

3. C. Pat McInally. The Cincinnati Bengals punter was first team All-Pro in 1981 with a league-best 45.4 yard average on 72 punts for the AFC champions. McInally also played wide receiver, catching six passes that year. He had 57 catches and five touchdowns in his 10-year career with the Bengals.

4. A. Matt Birk. Through 2011, Birk (Class of 1998) had been named to six Pro Bowls. All of those picks came with the Minnesota Vikings. Fellow Harvard alum Pat McInally (Class of 1976) punted in the Pro Bowl after the 1981 season, the same year he was named first team All-Pro.

5. D. St. Louis Rams. Harvard head coach Tim Murphy trekked to Minneapolis to see Rams linebacker Isaiah Kacyvenski and backup quarterback Ryan Fitzpatrick face the Vikings and fellow Harvard alum Pro Bowl center Matt Birk. The Rams won, 41-21.

6. False. Four players have been drafted from Harvard by the Patriots, and one saw playing time. Bobby Leo, a running back and receiver taken in the seventh round in 1967, played three games over two years. He caught a touchdown pass and had a 43-yard punt return, but three fumbles in his short stint sent him in search of other employment.

7. B. Wyndol Gray was a member of the first Celtics team in the forerunner of the NBA, the NBL. The Ohio native attended Bowling Green before joining the Navy in World War II. Afterward, he moved on to Harvard and had the distinction of being named an All-American at two different schools. He played the inaugural 1946-47 season with the Celtics and was third on the team in scoring (6.4 ppg) before being traded.

8. A. Boston College. The 82-70 win at Chestnut Hill over BC was the first victory by Harvard over a nationally ranked opponent in its 108-year history of men's basketball. Three days earlier, BC had beaten top-ranked North Carolina.

9. B. 1946. Led by Wyndol Gray, the Crimson reached the NCAA tournament in 1946. Harvard lost to Ohio State, 46-38.

10. True. The Crimson had appeared in the NCAA tournament but had never played in the NIT until 2011. The Crimson lost to Oklahoma State, 71-54.

11. Princeton. A playoff between the two schools ended with the Tigers beating the Crimson at the buzzer, 63-62. Princeton got the NCAA tournament's automatic bid.

12. C. Tufts.

13. True. The stadium was built in 1903 as a gift from the Class of 1879. Construction took less than five months and was done for the sum of $310,000.

14. A. Brown. The Crimson rallied to beat Brown, 24-17, before 18,898 fans in the first game under the lights at Harvard.

15. B. John Heisman. Pressed by President Teddy Roosevelt—a Harvard man—to "change the game or forsake it," Heisman, whose name would live on for the trophy named in his honor three decades later, developed the forward pass. Yale's Walter Camp had wanted to widen the field to open up the game, which would have rendered the new Harvard Stadium obsolete.

16. D. 1919. Coach Bob Fischer's team went 9-0-1, with a 7-6 win over Oregon in the Rose Bowl. At the time, Penn State was considered the East's best team, but years later when a committee was looking to name an official national champion for 1919, the committee looked at the record and picked Harvard. Bully!

17. C. Princeton. The Crimson was unscored upon until November. A 10-10 tie against Princeton on November 8 marked the only time the Crimson did not win in 1919. Yale scored the only other points against Harvard until the Rose Bowl on January 1, 1920, when Harvard beat Oregon, 7-6, in the only postseason bowl appearance in school history.

18. C. 30. Jennifer Botterill scored the deciding goal, and Angie Francisco tossed in a hat trick in a 6-5 victory over New Hampshire, Harvard's 30th in a row. Katey Stone's club finished the year with a 33-1 mark.

19. B. Brown. The 1898 match at Boston's Franklin Field was won by Brown, 6-0. It was Harvard's first-ever game.

20. B. 1859. Two years before the Civil War a 40-foot, six-oared pine shell with outriggers was raced for the first time against

Yale at Lake Quinsigamond in Worcester. And Harvard won. Naturally.

21. Four miles. Rowers from Harvard and Yale have competed at that distance since 1875. It began as two miles in 1852 and later switched to three.

22. D. Virginia. Though a significant day in sports, it was a mismatch on the field, with UVA winning, 47-0.

23. Keith Wright. Wright became just the second Crimson player to be Ivy League Player of the Year since it was first awarded in 1975. Coe Carrabino won the award as a junior in 1984. Both winners were junior power forwards at Harvard.

24. C. Emily Stauffer. An All-American at Harvard in 1995, 1996 and 1998, she took off 1997 to be with her brother and served as volunteer assistant coach. Matt Stauffer, an all-New England midfielder at Williams, lost his battle with leukemia in 1998. Emily Stauffer later spent two years with the New York Power in the Women's United Soccer Association while also teaching third grade.

25. C. Stanford. Co-captain Allison Feaster poured in 35 points and 13 rebounds to lead Harvard to a 71-67 NCAA first-round stunner on March 14, 1998—at Stanford, no less. Stanford had won 59 straight games at home and had been to the Final Four three straight years—but not in 1998.

26. C. Pat McInally. The wide receiver was on the Walter Camp 1974 All-American team. He spent more than a decade in the NFL, playing both wide receiver and punting for the Cincinnati Bengals. Before McInally, the last Harvard football All-American was Endicott Peabody in 1941.

27. B. Fencing. She was the school's first female NCAA individual titlist, in foil as a freshman in 2005. She later took time off to train for the Olympics, and it paid off with the silver medal in Beijing.

28. B. Polo Grounds. Infielder Eddie Grant batted .249 for the Philadelphia Phillies, Cincinnati Reds and New York Giants (1907-1915). "Harvard Eddie" was an infantry captain in France in World War I when he was killed by machine gun fire at the Battle of Meuse-Argonne in 1918. The plaque to him was erected in center field at the Polo Grounds in 1921 and disappeared in the fan frenzy after the last game there in 1957.

29. C. Maryland. Harvard went 15-0, the final win an 8-7 come-back victory in the championship game—played at Princeton, no less. Two-time All-American Charlotte Joslin completed her three-sport Harvard career with her 12th All-Ivy selection.

30. B. Squash. Harvard also claimed the men's and women's team titles.

'The Game'

1. B. 1875. Harvard blanked Yale in the first meeting on November 13, 1875, by the odd score of 4-0, with each score counting simply as one point.

2. A. 1913. Like their 2001 counterpart, the 1913 Crimson finished off a 9-0 season by beating Yale. Unlike 2001, though, the 1913 Harvard team was considered on par with any team in the country.

3. A. Clifton Dawson. Dawson broke a 34-year-old Ivy League mark with 4,841 rushing yards and also walked off with league marks for rushing touchdowns (60), career touchdowns (66), and career all-purpose yards (6,138). Dawson spent two years in the NFL before returning to Cambridge to attend Harvard Business School.

4. C. Men's soccer. The Crimson clinched the title with a scoreless tie against defending champion Yale. Harvard pulled off the double championship in a biting wind with a wind chill of minus 10.

5. B. 29. The Crimson scored 16 points in the final 42 seconds, creating the unforgettable headline in the Harvard *Crimson*: "Harvard Beats Yale, 29-29." Forty years later it was the name of an acclaimed documentary as well. The teams had gone into the final game with perfect conference records for the first time since 1909, and Yale was led by future NFL All-Pro running back Calvin Hill. Best tie ever.

6. Tommy Lee Jones. The Texan attended Harvard on a needs-based scholarship and graduated cum laude with an English degree in 1969. The big tackle was a roommate of Al Gore, for whom Jones gave the nominating speech at the 2000 Democratic Convention. Jones won the 1993 Academy Award for Best Supporting Actor for *The Fugitive*.

7. Harvard. The 16-7 win in New Haven also secured a share of the Ivy League title with Pennsylvania.

Northeastern

1. D. Maine. Northeastern lost its inaugural game, 29-13, and scored 13 again in an 11-point loss to Harvard. After six losses, the Huskies finally beat Harvard Law, and then lost their last seven.

2. C. 1981. The Huskies beat out Holy Cross to qualify for the NCAA tourney for the first time.

3. A. Fresno State. In the 12-team West bracket, the 11th-ranked Huskies upset the sixth-ranked Bulldogs, 55-53, in the 1981 NCAA tournament. (Howard was the only team seeded lower in the West.) Northeastern fell to third seed Utah in the round of 32 in El Paso. Indiana eventually won the tournament.

4. B. Boston YMCA. Everybody sing: "It's fun to play at the…"

5. False. Hall of Fame coach Jim Calhoun is the winningest coach in college history. He went 250-137 for a .646 winning percentage in the 1970s and 1980s. Dick Dukeshire had held the NU mark (204-100) during his coaching tenure from 1958 and 1971.

6. Five times they beat Holy Cross in the 1981 America East finals, Niagara in 1982, Canisius in 1984, and Boston University in 1985 and 1986. Jim Calhoun coached 14 years at Northeastern.

7. B. Harry Barnes. The former Northeastern star played a year for the San Diego Rockets in 1968-69 after being chosen in the fourth round.

8. D. Reggie Lewis. Lewis scored 2,709 points between 1983 and 1987 for Northeastern, ahead of Jose Barea (2,290), Pete Harris (2,167), and Matt Janning (1,836). The 22.2 points per game average by Lewis is likewise the best in school history.

9. C. 1966. Coach Jeanne Rowland's team came out gunning, beating Brandeis, 38-28, en route to a winning inaugural season.

10. D. Old Dominion. They needed just about every point and every ounce of energy in a 100-94 win over ODU in triple overtime on January 7, 2010.

11. True. And why not? Jim Calhoun was already the winningest coach in school history when he was inducted in 1985. Northeastern's secret was out, and he was pried away by Connecticut a year later.

12. Seven. The 2002-03 Huskies won six titles in the America East Conference and shared their first—and last—Atlantic 10 football title.

13. C. 2009. Northeastern dropped football after the 2009 season. The school informed the team a day after their final game, a 33-27 win at Rhode Island. Northeastern, which was drawing just 1,600 fans to home games, ended with a two-game winning streak.

14. C. 1966. Coach John Connelly's 18-6 Huskies made their way to Rosenblatt Stadium in Omaha for the College World Series. They stayed the minimum two games, losing to St. John's, 5-3, and dropping an 8-1 loser's bracket decision to Arizona. Ohio State won the '66 title.

15. Four: Les Williams (Blue Jays), Joe Maher (Yankees), Brandon McNelis (Angels) and Andrew Leenhouts (Marlins).

16. A. Mike Glavine. The Billerica product is brother of 300-game winner Tom Glavine. Mike was drafted as a junior by the Astros in the 93rd round in 1994. He did not sign and was drafted by the Indians the following year, this time in the 22nd round. Mike spent the final month of the 2003 season in the majors with Tom as a New York Met.

17. False. In fact, Carlos Pena is not in the Northeastern top 10 in homers. Pena, born in the Dominican Republic but raised in Massachusetts, started his career at Wright State in Ohio before coming to NU, so he had only two seasons between his first game with the Huskies and being taken in the first round of the 1998 draft by Texas. Pena is second in NU history in career slugging (.632) and on-base percentage (.462).

18. A. Cincinnati Bengals. Dan Ross set a Super Bowl record with 11 catches in Super Bowl XVI (a record since tied but not broken). The tight end's 104 yards receiving and two touchdowns helped the Bengals battle back, but the 49ers held on to win their first Super Bowl, 26-21.

19. D. 84. A Malden native, Dan Ross was an All-American at NU and set school marks for career receptions (153), receiving yards (2,343), and touchdown catches (13). He was taken in the second round of the 1979 draft and played tight end for four NFL teams, plus a year in the USFL.

20. B. Hammer throw. A member of the Northeastern Hall of Fame, Boris Djerassi won the 1975 NCAA title in the hammer

throw with an effort of 225 feet, 3 inches. He competed for his native Israel in the 1980 Olympics in Moscow.

Beanpot Challenge

1. Harvard, Northeastern, Boston University and Boston College, since 1953.

2. Harvard. The Crimson beat BU for the inaugural title, 7-4.

3. D. Cooney Weiland. He won the Stanley Cup with the 1929 Bruins and coached the 1941 Bruins to the Cup before spending 21 years at Harvard. He won five Beanpot titles and 315 games in all, claiming National Coach of the Year in 1955 and 1970.

4. Northeastern, in overtime against Boston College in 1980.

5. A. Bill Cleary. A 1960 hockey gold medal winner for the U.S. in Squaw Valley, he set the Beanpot record in 1955 for goals in a period (4), game (5), and tournament (7). He turned down an offer by the Canadiens to stay at Harvard. Cleary coached the Crimson for 22 years before stepping down in 1990 as coach to serve another decade as athletic director.

6. Boston University. The tally through 2011: BU 29, BC 16, Harvard 10, Northeastern 4.

7. A. 1979. Northeastern blanked Harvard for the first women's title, 4-0.

8. UMass-Amherst

College Knowledge

1. B. Chelsea native Ed King played guard and defensive end for Buffalo in the All-America Football Conference (1948-49) and the NFL's Baltimore Colts (1950). He defeated Mike Dukakis for governor in 1978 and then lost to Dukakis in 1982.

2. D. MIT. Henry Steinbrenner was a world-class track-and-field star and first in his class of 1927. He became a shipping magnate of the Great Lakes and the domineering father who spawned the brutish clan of the Evil Empire.

3. B. Boston University. The Pats played at Nickerson Field their first three seasons in the AFL (1960-62).

4. A. Boston College. The Boston Patriots played at Alumni Stadium in Chestnut Hill in 1969.

5. C. Harvard hosted the Patriots in their inaugural season in the NFL in 1970, following the merger with the AFL. In 1971 the Boston Patriots moved to Foxboro and became known as the New England Patriots.

6. D. Greco-Roman Wrestling. Jim Peckham later served as Emerson's athletic director and then as head coach at Harvard.

7. A. Baseball. With Division III Lesley already having men's and women's teams in basketball, cross-country, soccer, tennis, track and volleyball, it made sense for the Lynx to add baseball to sync up with the softball program.

8. The Jumbos. A trustee at Tufts, P.T. Barnum gave the stuffed remains of the famously large elephant known as Jumbo to Tufts, as well as funds to build Barnum Hall. A fire in the building reduced Jumbo to ashes in 1974, but those remains are kept in a peanut butter jar in the athletic director's office.

9. B. 1945. Tufts lost to NYU in the 1945 NCAA tournament, 59-44. Tufts played in the third-place game as well and fell to Kentucky, 66-56.

10. Bentley College. Taken by Carolina in the seventh and final round of the 2008 draft, Mackenzy Bernadeau is the only player drafted out of Bentley to ever make an NFL roster.

11. D. Tufts University. Travel restrictions made Tufts stand in for Florida in the midst of World War II.

12. B. Emmanuel. The 1,700-student Catholic college uses the facility named after the Pittsburgh Pirates great for its softball, soccer and lacrosse games. Roberto Clemente Field is about a 15-minute walk from Fenway Park.

13. D. Judges. Division III Brandeis derives its mascot's name from famed Supreme Court Justice Oliver Wendell Holmes Jr., who served on the bench with Louis Brandeis, for whom the school is named. The Brandeis College mascot is Ollie the Owl.

14. Former Celtics K.C. Jones (1967-70), Bob Brannum (1970-86) and Chris Ford (2001-03) all served as head basketball coaches at Brandeis.

15. A. Beacons. Not to be confused with the Minutemen of UMass-Amherst, the Beacons are named for the lighthouses that guided ships into Boston Harbor in the black of night. Boston's historic Beacon Hill neighborhood is named for the

beacon that stood there in the 1700s before the peaks were shorn off and houses built.

16. The Codfish Bowl. UMass-Boston inherited the event from Boston State College in 1982. Some three dozen schools have taken part since its founding in 1965 (the Beanpot college hockey tourney is 13 years older). UMass-Boston has appeared in the event more often than any school, winning the Codfish Bowl in 1983, 1997 and 2007.

17. C. MIT. Thomas Pelham Curtis threw himself across the finish line to beat Great Britain's Grantley Goulding at the finish line at the 1896 Olympics in Athens. Officials stated that the electrical engineering student won by five centimeters.

18. B. California Angels (as they were then known). Alan Dopfel spent three years in the minors, reaching Class AAA Salt Lake City. In 1975 spring training he fanned Oakland's Reggie Jackson, but A's all-star Joe Rudi hit one out of sight in the same game. After being sent back to the minors, he retired to work at IBM.

19. C. Ron Hainsey. The Connecticut native was drafted by the Montreal Canadiens with the 13th overall pick in 2000. He was picked up off waivers by the Columbus Blue Jackets, establishing himself as a solid two-way defenseman. Hainsey later signed a contract with the Atlanta Thrashers, now the Winnipeg Jets.

20. C. Holy Cross. Jon Norris, who was named to the Pro Bowl his first seven seasons, was drafted by the Patriots in the fourth round of the 1964 AFL draft. Norris was also chosen by the Green Bay Packers in the second round of the NFL draft that year, but Norris stayed local.

The Patriots

Patriots Basics

1. True or false? The 2011 Patriots were first in the AFC in passing yards per game on offense and last in the conference in passing yards per game on defense.

2. Ron Gronkowski set an NFL record for most touchdowns by a tight end in 2011. How many TDs did Gronk catch?
   A. 11
   B. 14
   C. 17
   D. 20

3. In 1993 a new Patriots logo replaced the one that had been on team helmets since 1961. What was the nickname of the team's original incarnation?

4. Including playoffs, which team have the Patriots defeated more often than any other?

    A. Buffalo Bills

    B. Indianapolis Colts

    C. Miami Dolphins

    D. New York Jets

5. Who is the only Patriots guard other than John Hannah to earn a Pro Bowl bid since the 1970 merger?

    A. Sean Farrell

    B. Logan Mankins

    C. Stephen Neal

    D. Ron Wooten

6. True or False? The Patriots hosted the first sporting event at Gillette Stadium.

7. The Patriots set the record for most consecutive playoff wins in NFL history. How many postseason wins in a row did the Pats reel off?

    A. 6

    B. 8

    C. 10

    D. 12

8. True or false? The Patriots have never had a losing record under Bill Belichick.

9. The latest matchup of undefeated teams in NFL history occurred on November 4, 2007 between the Pats (7-0) and which 8-0 team?

    A. Green Bay Packers

    B. Indianapolis Colts

    C. New York Giants

    D. San Diego Chargers

10. Who was the first Patriot to kick soccer style?

    A. Gino Cappelletti

    B. Charlie Gogolak

    C. Pete Gogolak

    D. John Smith

11. On October 10, 2010, the Patriots became the first team to ever score touchdowns five different ways in a 41-14 rout in Miami. Name the five ways they found the end zone.

12. What school hosted the first college game ever played at Gillette Stadium in 2010?

13. Who returned a fumble for a touchdown in the 1996 AFC Championship Game to propel the Patriots to the Super Bowl?

14. What Patriot converted the first successful drop kick in the NFL in 65 years?

15. What 2011 Patriot is the son of a Pro Football Hall of Famer?

16. Rumors of the Patriots relocating across the country in 1993 resulted from the Sullivan family selling the Pats to owners from what city?

17. This former Kent State quarterback set the Patriots franchise record for punt return average in a season and longest punt return in 2010. Who is he?
    A. Troy Brown
    B. Julian Edelman
    C. Brandon Tate
    D. Wes Welker

18. The Patriots once made the playoffs with their leading scorer recording 21 points for the season. What year was it?
    A. 1960
    B. 1976
    C. 1982
    D. 1987

19. The "tuck rule" famously went in favor of the Patriots in the 2001 playoffs, but the same call went against the Patriots a month earlier against which team?
    A. New York Jets
    B. Oakland Raiders
    C. San Diego Chargers
    D. St. Louis Rams

20. Under new head coach Bill Parcells, the 1993 Patriots had a losing mark but won in overtime on the final play of the season to finish the year with a winning streak of how many games?

21. Who held the record for wins by a Patriots head coach before it was broken by Bill Belichick?
    A. Raymond Berry
    B. Ron Ehrhardt
    C. Mike Holovak
    D. Lou Saban

22. Which is the only state besides Massachusetts to host a Patriots regular-season game?
    A. Alabama
    B. Arkansas
    C. Connecticut
    D. Rhode Island

23. Who was chosen as "captain" of the 50th anniversary Patriots team in 2009?
    A. Tom Brady
    B. Troy Brown
    C. Nick Buoniconti
    D. Gino Cappelletti

24. The biggest blowout in Patriots history occurred during an October 2009 snowstorm against the same team the Pats had beaten in the coldest game in team history six years earlier. What warm-weather team twice suffered at the hands of the Pats and the cruel New England elements?

A. Arizona Cardinals

B. Jacksonville Jaguars

C. Miami Dolphins

D. Tennessee Titans

25. How many consecutive weeks did the Patriots win while scoring 30 points or more to finish the 2010 season?

26. Who took over at quarterback for the Patriots after Tom Brady was lost for the 2008 season in the first game of the year?

27. Name the only two quarterbacks the Patriots have taken with the first overall pick in the NFL draft.

28. Who was the first Patriot to be named Associated Press Offensive Rookie of the Year?

A. Drew Bledsoe

B. Stanley Morgan

C. Leonard Russell

D. John Stephens

29. True or False? In 2008 Jerod Mayo became the only Patriot to be named Defensive Rookie of the Year.

30. Adam Vinatieri was originally recruited to kick at West Point, but he left after two weeks and wound up kicking at which college closer to home?

A. North Dakota State

B. South Dakota State

C. St. Copious of Northern Nebraska

D. Valdosta State

31. The 2003-04 Patriots put together the longest winning streak of regular season and postseason games in NFL history. How long was it?

A. 16 games

B. 18 games

C. 21 games

D. 24 games

32. At the start of the Patriots' legendary run to consecutive Super Bowls, the Patriots opened the 2003 season by getting shut out by whom?

A. Buffalo Bills

B. Miami Dolphins

C. New York Jets

D. Pittsburgh Steelers

33. The Patriots were held to a single touchdown by Cincinnati on December 12, 1993, yet New England won the game at frigid Foxboro. What was the final score?

    A. 7-0

    B. 7-2

    C. 7-3

    D. 7-6

34. Who recovered the most fumbles in Patriots history?

    A. Bob Dee

    B. Willie McGinest

    C. Steve Nelson

    D. Andre Tippett

35. Stephen Gostkowski was a walk-on kicker at Memphis, but he was at the school on a partial scholarship in which sport?

36. Patriots tight end Rob Gronkowski, who caught 10 touchdown passes as a rookie in 2010, is part of just the ninth brothers trio to appear in the NFL at the same time, and the first since 1992. Name at least one of Rob's NFL brothers and the position he plays.

37. Due to numerous player injuries in 2004, Bill Belichick was forced to use wide receiver Troy Brown as a defensive back. How many interceptions did Brown make to help the Pats defend their NFL title?

A. 0

B. 1

C. 3

D. 4

38. Between 1991-93 the Patriots lost how many games when allowing six points or less?

39. True or false? The year the Patriots went undefeated until the Super Bowl, they also won all their preseason games.

40. From what team did the Patriots acquire Randy Moss from in 2007?

A. Minnesota Vikings

B. Oakland Raiders

C. Tennessee Titans

D. Washington Redskins

41. True or false? During their 16-0 season the Patriots did not have a 1,000-yard rusher.

42. Who scored more points for the 2007 Patriots: wide receiver Randy Moss or kicker Stephen Gostkowski?

43. True or false? In the first 40 years since the AFL-NFL merger, the Patriots did not have a game end in a tie.

44. How many times did Matt Cassel lead the Patriots to 40 points during his season as quarterback?
   A. 0
   B. 2
   C. 4
   D. 6

45. True or false? A 2010 playoff defeat marked the first time the Patriots had ever lost to the Jets in the postseason.

46. Through 2011, can you name the last Patriots head coach who was not employed as a head coach by the Jets?

47. Bill Belichick began his pro coaching career as a $25 per-week-special assistant for which NFL team?

A. Baltimore Colts

B. Detroit Lions

C. New York Giants

D. New York Jets

48. How many games did the Patriots win in Bill Belichick's first season with the team?

A. 5

B. 7

C. 9

D. 11

49. Who was New England's first-round draft choice in 2011?

50. Who set New England's record for rushing yards in a season in 2004?

A. Terry Allen

B. Corey Dillon

C. Curtis Martin

D. Antowain Smith

51. The franchise record for the most 100-yard receiving games is 38. Who holds that mark?

A. Troy Brown

B. Irving Fryar

C. Stanley Morgan

D. Wes Welker

52. The Patriots have employed one barefoot kicker in their history. Name him.

53. Who is the only Patriot with 100 career sacks?
    A. Teddy Bruschi
    B. Willie McGinest
    C. Andre Tippett
    D. Mike Vrabel

54. What country is Patriots punter Zoltan Mesko from?
    A. Croatia
    B. Hungary
    C. Latvia
    D. Romania

55. The day before the Red Sox began their legendary three-games-to-none comeback against the New York Yankees in the 2003 Championship Series, which New York team did the Patriots beat in Foxboro?

56. Which year among the championship seasons 2001, 2003 and 2004 did the Patriots win a regular-season game in the same stadium where they later won that year's Super Bowl?

57. In the last seven games of 2003, the Patriots had how many shutouts?

58. When Tom Brady tossed 50 touchdown passes in 2007, how many interceptions did he throw?

A. 8

B. 11

C. 14

D. 17

59. Matt Cassell was sacked 47 times with the Patriots in 2008, but that is still a dozen short of the club record set by which New England quarterback?

A. Tom Brady

B. Tony Eason

C. Steve Grogan

D. Jim Plunkett

60. What is the longest number of seasons the Patriots have gone without a winning season?

A. 5

B. 7

C. 9

D. 11

61. Which Patriots quarterback holds the NFL single-season record for the most pass attempts?

A. Drew Bledsoe

B. Tom Brady

C. Tony Eason

D. Babe Parilli

62. In three successive years (2008-10), the Patriots played games in which it snowed heavily throughout. They plowed under their competitors in those games by a composite score of 142-14. Name the three teams they buried.

63. En route to surpassing 30,000 career passing yards in 2009, who did Tom Brady pass as the all-time Patriots leader in that category?

64. Since quarterbacks handle the ball more than any other player, they also tend to fumble more than any other player. Not surprisingly, the three longest-tenured Pats QBs have the most career fumble recoveries. But who has the most career fumble recoveries by a Patriots defender?
    A. Mike Haynes
    B. Willie McGinest
    C. Andre Tippett
    D. Vince Wilfork

65. True or false? The Patriots made the playoffs the year before Tom Brady emerged as starting quarterback.

66. What are the fewest yards rushing allowed by the Patriots in a game?

    A. -2

    B. 2

    C. 12

    D. 22

67. Through 2011, the last time the Patriots lost more than two in a row was 2002, when they dropped four straight. Name two of the four teams the Pats lost to in that streak.

68. The 2011 Giants handed the Patriots their first regular-season loss in Foxboro in how many games?

    A. 16

    B. 18

    C. 20

    D. 22

69. Patriots kicker Stephen Gostkowski set a record for most points after touchdown in a season in 2007. How many PATs did he make?

    A. 62

    B. 66

    C. 70

    D. 74

70. The Patriots were the first NFL team to ever draft a wide receiver with the first overall pick. Whom did they choose?

A. Troy Brown

B. Irving Fryar

C. Terry Glenn

D. Stanley Morgan

71. In 2002 and 2003 linebacker Tedy Bruschi scored two touchdowns each year on interceptions. How many total interceptions did he have in those two seasons combined?

A. 5

B. 7

C. 10

D. 13

72. Who coached the Patriots immediately before Bill Belichick?

73. The worst season in Patriots history was 1990, when the Pats went 1-15. Who was the coach?

A. Raymond Berry

B. Dick McPherson

C. Bill Parcells

D. Rod Rust

74. Before the Patriots brokered a deal to build a new stadium in Foxboro, with which city did owner Bob Kraft have a tentative deal to relocate the team?

75. Which coach replaced Bill Parcells after Super Bowl XXXI?

76. Which team did the Patriots beat for their first postseason win in the NFL in 1985?
A. Buffalo Bills
B. Cleveland Browns
C. Miami Dolphins
D. New York Jets

77. Who did the Patriots beat in the AFC Championship Game to reach their first Super Bowl?
A. Jacksonville Jaguars
B. Miami Dolphins
C. Oakland Raiders
D. San Diego Chargers

78. What year did Foxboro switch from artificial turf to natural grass?
A. 1971
B. 1981
C. 1991
D. 2001

79. Who holds the Patriots record for consecutive games played?
A. Troy Brown
B. Gino Cappelletti
C. Raymond Clayborn
D. John Hannah

80. Who was the first person inducted into the Patriots Hall of Fame in 1991?

A. Bruce Armstrong

B. Steve Grogan

C. John Hannah

D. Stanley Morgan

81. True or false? Drew Bledsoe is a member of the Patriots Hall of Fame.

82. Name the Patriots running back who set a club record with most yards per carry in a season in 2010.

83. True or false? Wes Welker had more receptions in his first year with the Patriots than he did in three years with Miami and San Diego.

84. How many points did the 2007 Pats score to establish a league record?

A. 496

B. 517

C. 566

D. 587

85. The 2010 Patriots set an NFL mark for fewest turnovers. How low did they go?

    A. 10

    B. 13

    C. 26

    D. 19

86. Is Foxboro Stadium closer to Boston or Providence?

87. In 2010 cornerback Devin McCourty became the fourth Patriots rookie named to the Pro Bowl. Which of the following Pats did *not* make the Pro Bowl trip as a rook?

    A. Mike Haynes

    B. Curtis Martin

    C. John Stephens

    D. Andre Tippett

88. Before Tom Brady, who was the last Patriots passer to lead the NFL in touchdown passes in a season?

    A. Drew Bledsoe

    B. Tony Eason

    C. Steve Grogan

    D. Babe Parilli

89. Who is the only Patriots coach to never lose a season opener?

A. Bill Belichick

B. Raymond Berry

C. Chuck Fairbanks

D. Bill Parcells

90. In 1994 Drew Bledsoe threw 27 interceptions to tie the club record set by whom?

A. Drew Bledsoe

B. Steve Grogan

C. Babe Parilli

D. Jim Plunkett

91. After the 2011 season opener, Tom Brady said the 4 p.m. start the next week for the team's home opener would allow fans to "start drinking early. Get nice and rowdy." What team came to Foxboro to face the Pats and their "lubed up" fans in the 2011 home opener?

A. Buffalo Bills

B. Miami Dolphins

C. New York Jets

D. San Diego Chargers

92. What is the smallest home crowd to see Patriots in franchise history?

A. 6,791

B. 8,446

C. 9,398

D. 11,878

93. What year did the Patriots first sell out every seat before the season began?

A. 1985

B. 1990

C. 1995

D. 2000

94. True or false? The Patriots have never hosted a Thanksgiving Day game.

95. Who led the Patriots to a 2-12 record a year after serving as starting quarterback for a team that reached the Super Bowl?

A. Joe Kapp

B. Jim Plunkett

C. Babe Parilli

D. Marc Wilson

96. Who kicked the longest field goal in Patriots history?

A. Matt Bahr

B. Tony Franklin

C. Stephen Gostkowski

D. Adam Vinatieri

97. This future Patriots Pro Bowler showed New England what he could do as a Miami rookie by becoming the first player in NFL history to return both a punt and a kickoff and kick a field goal and an extra point in the same game. Who was this multitalented star?

98. Which Patriot returned the most interceptions for touchdowns in his career?

A. Ted Bruschi

B. Raymond Clayborn

C. Mike Haynes

D. Ty Law

99. What is the only original AFL team the Patriots have never faced in the playoffs, through 2011?

A. Buffalo Bills

B. Denver Broncos

C. Kansas City Chiefs/Dallas Texans

D. Tennessee Titans/Houston Oilers

100. The Patriots went through four head coaches between 1989 and 1993. Name three of them.

101. Bill Belichick is among the winningest playoff coaches in pro football history. Through 2011, which legendary coach has the most playoff victories?

A. Bill Belichick

B. Tom Landry

C. Vince Lombardi

D. Chuck Noll

102. Through 2011, how many times has Bill Belichick won at least 14 games in a season?

103. Who was the Baltimore Ravens kicker whose last-second field goal miss allowed the Patriots to win the 2011 AFC title?

A. Billy Cundiff

B. Scott Norwood

C. Jim O'Brien

D. Matt Stover

104. What Patriots defensive back tied for the NFL lead in interceptions in 2011?

105. Who set the Patriots record with 4.5 sacks in a game in 2011?

A. Mark Anderson

B. Andre Carter

C. Rob Ninkovich

D. Vince Wilfork

106. What longtime Patriots defensive lineman picked up the first two interceptions and the first touchdown of his NFL career in 2011?

107. True or false? The opening quarter of Super Bowl XLVI marked the first time in seven New England Super Bowls that the Patriots were called for a safety.

108. How many Patriots starters were the same on offense and defense against the Giants in Super Bowl XLII as compared with the rematch in Super Bowl XLVI?

A. 0

B. 2

C. 5

D. 10

109. Which city hosted Super Bowl XLVI between the Giants and Patriots?

A. Houston

B. Indianapolis

C. New Orleans

D. Phoenix

110. Tom Brady set a Super Bowl record for consecutive completions in Super Bowl XLVI. How many passes in a row did he complete?

A. 9

B. 13

C. 16

D. 20

Answers on pages 179-190

The Brady Bunch (of Questions)

1. Tom Brady started the 2011 season with the most passing yards in a three-week span in NFL history. For how many yards did he throw in the first three weeks of 2011?

   A. 1,001

   B. 1,221

   C. 1,257

   D. 1,327

2. In what round and from what school was Tom Brady chosen by the Patriots in the 2000 NFL draft?

3. Which of the following players was *not* drafted ahead of Tom Brady by the Patriots in the 2000 NFL draft?

   A. Adrian Klemm

   B. David Nugent

   C. J.R. Redmond

   D. Dave Stachleski

4. How many yards did Tom Brady average per game in 2007?

   A. 250

   B. 275

   C. 300

   D. 325

5. What year did Tom Brady earn Associated Press Comeback Player of the Year Award?

6. Tom Brady was drafted out of high school to play baseball by the Montreal Expos at what position?

7. Against which division rival did Tom Brady record the first perfect passer rating in Patriots history in 2007?

8. Whose hit knocked out Drew Bledsoe and brought in Tom Brady in 2001?
   A. John Abraham
   B. James Farrior
   C. Mo Lewis
   D. Ray Lewis

9. Which team did Tom Brady beat in his first NFL start?
   A. Buffalo Bills
   B. Indianapolis Colts
   C. Miami Dolphins
   D. New York Jets

Answers on pages 190-191

Your Father's Patriots

1. The Patriots had one offensive and one defensive player named to the NFL's All-1980s team, plus a third was named second team. Name two of the three. Hint: all three are Hall of Famers.

2. Which team beat the Patriots with a last-minute touchdown in the 1976 AFC playoffs in one of the most controversial games in team history?
   A. Baltimore Colts
   B. Houston Oilers
   C. Pittsburgh Steelers
   D. Oakland Raiders

3. True or false? The Patriots won the last game at Baltimore's Memorial Stadium before the Colts up and moved in the middle of the night to Indianapolis after the 1983 season.

4. Which school did the Patriots draft quarterback Steve Grogan out of in 1975?
   A. Alabama
   B. Kansas
   C. Kansas State
   D. Kentucky

5. Name the first former NFL team the Patriots defeated in the regular season following the merger between the NFL and AFL.

   A. Baltimore Colts

   B. Cleveland Browns

   C. New York Giants

   D. St. Louis Cardinals

6. New England's fortunes changed with the drafting of guard John Hannah, running back Sam "Bam" Cunningham and wide receiver Darryl Stingley in the first round of which year's draft?

   A. 1971

   B. 1973

   C. 1975

   D. 1977

7. Who debuted in the NFL at quarterback for the Patriots in the first game played in Foxboro?

8. Who was the Oakland Raiders defender whose vicious hit on Darryl Stingley in a 1978 preseason game left the Patriots wide receiver paralyzed?

9. To which team did the Patriots trade Jim Plunkett for an NFL quarterback, two 1976 first-round picks and a 1977 second-round pick?

   A. New York Giants

   B. Oakland Raiders

   C. San Francisco 49ers

   D. Washington Redskins

10. True or false? The Patriots beat the Tampa Bay Buccaneers in the last game of 1976 to assure the Bucs of the only 0-14 season in NFL history.

11. Who kicked the field goal for the Patriots to beat Miami in the snow in 1982 after the area where the field goal would be spotted was cleared by a snowplow?

12. With New England preparing for the AFC playoffs in 1978, Chuck Fairbanks abruptly announced he was leaving the Patriots to coach at which university?
    A. Alabama
    B. Colorado
    C. Nebraska
    D. Oklahoma

13. Which running back has held the franchise record for career rushing yards for more than three decades?

14. The first two Patriots with more than 1,000 yards receiving were on the 1979 squad. Name both receivers.

15. This defensive back celebrated his team-record 111th straight start by scoring the first touchdown of his career on an interception return. Name him.

16. What company did late 1980s owner Victor Kiam run in addition to the Patriots?

    A. Gillete Razors

    B. Kraft Foods

    C. Remington Razors

    D. Schaefer Beer

17. By how many wins did the Patriots improve from 1975 to 1976?

    A. 2

    B. 4

    C. 6

    D. 8

18. What year did the team change from the Boston Patriots to the New England Patriots?

    A. 1969

    B. 1970

    C. 1971

    D. 1972

19. What area designation did the Patriots initially prefer over "New England"?

20. In 1978, the first year of the 16-game schedule, the Patriots set an NFL record for most rushing yards in a season. How many yards did they pile up?

A. 1,961

B. 2,344

C. 2,801

D. 3,165

Answers on pages 191-193

The Super Bowl Challenge

1. Who took the first snap in a Super Bowl for the Patriots?

2. Who scored the first points by a Patriots in Super Bowl history barely a minute into Super Bowl XX?

   A. Tony Eason

   B. Tony Franklin

   C. Steve Grogan

   D. Adam Vinatieri

3. Super Bowl XLVI between the Patriots and Giants was a "rematch" of a previous Super Bowl pairing. How many other times in Super Bowl history have teams lined up against each other more than once?

   A. 0

   B. 2

   C. 4

   D. 6

4. Who was the holder for both Super Bowl winning kicks by Adam Vinatieri?

   A. Brooks Barnard

   B. Drew Bledsoe

   C. Tom Brady

   D. Ken Walter

5. Who spent the day of Super Bowl XXXIX calling 30 different high school, junior college and college coaches to thank them for their support, then went out and tied a record to help win the big game for the Patriots?

6. The first three Super Bowls the Patriots played in were all held in the same city and stadium. Name the city and the stadium.

7. In what city did the Pats win their third championship at Super Bowl XXXIX?
   A. Houston
   B. Jacksonville
   C. Miami
   D. New Orleans

8. Whose interception in the closing seconds secured New England's victory in Super Bowl XXXIX?
   A. Tedy Bruschi
   B. Rodney Harrison
   C. Asante Samuel
   D. Mike Vrabel

9. The Patriots won three Super Bowls between the 2001 and 2004 seasons. Which team won the other Super Bowl in that span, following the 2002 season?
   A. Baltimore Ravens
   B. Pittsburgh Steelers
   C. St. Louis Rams
   D. Tampa Bay Buccaneers

Answers on pages 193-194

Your Grandfather's Patriots

1. The founders of the American Football League considered themselves members of an exclusive society. What was their nickname for themselves?

    A. All Fool's League

    B. The Foolish Club

    C. The Schmucks

    D. Skull and Bones Society

2. The Boston Patriots were the only American Football League team to have a public stock offering when they formed in 1960. How much did one of the original 120,000 shares of Pats stock have cost?

    A. $1.25

    B. $2.50

    C. $4.75

    D. $25

3. Which Massachusetts native scored the Patriots' first-ever touchdown in 1960?

    A. Ron Burton

    B. Nick Buoniconti

    C. Gino Cappelletti

    D. Jim Colclough

4. Who was the all-time leading scorer in AFL history with 1,130 points?

    A. Ron Burton

    B. Nick Buoniconti

    C. Gino Cappelletti

    D. Jim Nance

5. Jim Nance is the Pats all-time leader in rushing touchdowns. How many did he score?
    A. 25
    B. 35
    C. 45
    D. 55

6. The Patriots reached the postseason once in the American Football League. Whom did they play in the championship game?
    A. Buffalo Bills
    B. Houston Oilers
    C. Oakland Raiders
    D. San Diego Chargers

7. What famous son of Massachusetts received a 1961 letter from Patriots head coach Lou Saban asking if he would like to play receiver for the Pats?

8. Where was the first Patriots training camp held in 1960?
    A. Bryant University in Rhode Island
    B. Holy Cross in Worcester
    C. Phillips Academy in Andover
    D. University of Massachusetts at Amherst

9. What emblem was on the original Patriots helmet in 1960?

   A. Block letters spelling "Patriots"

   B. Flying Elvis

   C. Pat the Patriot hiking a ball

   D. Tricorned hat and uniform number

10. Against which team did the Patriots gain the franchise's first ever win?

    A. Denver Broncos

    B. Houston Oilers

    C. Los Angeles Chargers

    D. New York Titans

11. The Patriots retired the uniform numbers of how many players who spent the majority of their careers with the club in the American Football League?

12. In the decade the American Football League was in existence, the Patriots had two league MVPs. Who were they?

13. Arrange these stadiums in the order in which the Patriots used them, using 1 for first, 2 for second, etc.

    A. Alumni Stadium

    B. Fenway Park

    C. Harvard Stadium

    D. Nickerson Field

14. Professional football had been played by various teams before the Patriots came into existence. Which of the following was *not* a Boston-based football club prior to 1950?

A. Boston Braves

B. Boston Redskins

C. Boston Red Sox

D. Boston Yanks

15. Which happened first in team history: the Patriots shut out an opponent or they got shut out?

16. The Miami Dolphins were the AFL's first expansion team. Did the Pats win or lose their first game with the Fish in 1966?

17. If the Patriots had won their last game of the 1966 season, they would have forced a playoff for the AFL East title and could have wound up in Super Bowl I. Which team beat the Pats in the last game of the year?

A. Buffalo Bills

B. Kansas City Chiefs

C. New York Jets

D. Oakland Raiders

18. Who drew the iconic "Pat the Patriot" while working as a *Boston Globe* cartoonist in 1959?

    A. Mike Barnicle

    B. Phil Bissell

    C. Will McDonough

    D. Billy Sullivan

19. True or false?Patriots kicker and ball catcher extraordinaire Gino Cappelletti was the all-time leading field goal kicker at the University of Minnesota.

20. Toughest question of the bunch: Name at least one member of the WEEI radio team for the first Patriots game in 1960.

Answers on pages 194-196

Pats Firsts

1. The Boston Patriots played the first game in American Football League history on September 9, 1960. Who was their opponent?
   A. Buffalo Bills
   B. Denver Broncos
   C. Houston Oilers
   D. New York Titans

2. Who took the first snap in the first Patriots game in 1961?
   A. Gino Cappelletti
   B. Tom Greene
   C. Babe Parilli
   D. Butch Songin

3. Which year did the Patriots cheerleaders hit the sidelines for the first time?
   A. 1960
   B. 1967
   C. 1977
   D. 1987

4. Who was the first career Patriot inducted into the Pro Football Hall of Fame?

5. In 2009 the Patriots played their first regular-season game on foreign soil at London's Wembley Stadium. Which NFC team was the opponent?

   A. Atlanta Falcons

   B. New Orleans Saints

   C. New York Giants

   D. Tampa Bay Buccaneers

6. Which team did the Patriots beat for their first-ever overtime win after 10 games and 14 years of fruitless OT?

   A. Miami Dolphins

   B. Pittsburgh Steelers

   C. Tampa Bay Buccaneers

   D. Washington Redskins

7. Who was the first Patriot to rush for 1,000 yards in a season?

   A. Ron Burton

   B. Sam "Bam" Cunningham

   C. Larry Garron

   D. Jim Nance

8. Who was the first Patriot to rush for more than 100 yards in a game?

   A. Ron Burton

   B. Larry Garron

   C. Alan Miller

   D. Jim Nance

Answers on pages 196-197

Patriots Answers

Patriots Basics

1. True. NFC South champion New Orleans, courtesy of record-setter Drew Brees, was the only team to surpass New England's 5,084 yards passing. NFC North winner Green Bay was the only defense to exceed the 4,703 yards piled up against the Pats. New England led the AFC in both categories by more than 500 yards.

2. 17. Rob Gronkowski's 14th TD catch of the year broke a second-half tie with the Redskins as well as the record for TDs by a tight end set by San Diego's Antonio Gates in 2004. Gronk hauled in three more touchdowns over the final three weeks.

3. C. Pat the Patriot. The beloved Revolutionary War-era big man posed in a three-point stance in his tricorned hat.

4. A. Buffalo Bills. Through 2011, the Pats were 62-41-1 against the Bills, dating back to the first year of the AFL in 1960. The Jets were second, with the teams dead even after 103 games, including a tie. The Colts, whom the Pats did not play for the first time until 1970, were third. Fourth belonged to the Dolphins, against whom the Pats have a losing mark due to a 10-21 stretch from 1970-85.

5. B. Logan Mankins. Mankins was named to the Pro Bowl for the first time in 2007, making him the only Patriots guard so honored through 2011 by the NFL—other than, of course, Hall of Famer John Hannah (a nine-time Pro Bowler).

6. False. The New England Revolution soccer team opened the place on May 11, 2002. The Patriots played their first preseason game there against the Eagles on September 1, and the first regular-season game was on Monday night, September 9, a 30-14 win over the Steelers in which the Patriots unfurled their world championship flag.

7. C. 10. The Pats won every playoff game they played from the 2001 postseason's "tuck rule" game through their 2005 first-round win over Jacksonville. The streak, which broke the mark held by Vince Lombardi's 1960s Packers, ended in Denver.

8. False. The Pats went 5-11 in Bill Belichick's first season with the club in 2000.

9. B. Indianapolis Colts. The Pats won, 24-20, en route to their 16-0 season.

10. C. Charlie Gogolak. The Hungarian Gogolak kicking fraternity—Charlie and his brother Pete—brought soccer-style kicking to the pro ranks. Charlie was successful just 55 percent of the time in three seasons with the Pats (1970-72). Older brother Pete brought soccer style to the pro ranks, but he kicked for Buffalo and the Giants.

11. Kick return (Brandon Tate), rushing (BenJarvus Green-Ellis), receiving (Danny Woodhead from Tom Brady), blocked field goal return (Kyle Arrington) and interception return (Patrick Chung).

12. The University of Massachusetts. The Amherst school hosted the first "Colonial Clash in Foxboro," but the Minutemen lost to New Hampshire, 39-13, in front of 32,848.

13. Otis Smith. His 47-yard return of a fumble by James Stewart in the closing minutes ended Jacksonville's potential game-tying drive.

14. Doug Flutie. The 43-year-old Boston College icon called it a career with a drop kick for an extra point in the Pats' 28-26 win against Miami on January 2, 2006. Even Bill Belichick, who knew the last dropkick PAT had been in 1941, broke out a big smile.

15. Matthew Slater. The wide receiver and special teams player is the son of Jackie Slater, who spent 20 seasons with the Rams and has been enshrined in Canton since 2001. Matthew is one of six sons of Hall of Fame players to be drafted in the NFL (fifth round by the Patriots in 2008).

16. St. Louis. After the Cardinals moved to Arizona, St. Louis had no football team, and new Patriots owner James Orthwein went so far as to create a logo for the "St. Louis Stallions." The Pats stayed, of course, and were bought by Robert Kraft. A Stallions cap is on display at the Patriots Hall of Fame in Foxboro.

17. B. Julian Edelman. The leading passer—and rusher—at Kent State in 2008, his 15.3-yard punt return average in 2010 was tops in Patriots history and the best since Troy Brown's 14.2 in 2001. Edelman's 94-yard punt return for a touchdown in the final game of 2010 broke the record of 89 yards set by Hall of Famer Mike Haynes in 1976.

18. C. 1982. The top scorer was left-footed British kicker John Smith. He recorded five extra points and six field goals; one was very controversial because a snow plow cleared a path moments before he kicked it. The Pats went 5-4 in the shortened 1982 schedule and squeaked into the expanded playoffs despite being 21st in the NFL in scoring (143 points).

19. A. The New York Jets. The call in the December 2, 2001, game was reversed in New York's favor, but the Patriots won by a point anyway.

20. Four. Michael Timpson's 36-yard touchdown catch in OT beat Miami and salvaged a 5-11 season out of what had been a 1-11 disaster in early December.

21. C. Mike Holovak. He won 52 times between 1961 and 1968, a mark Bill Belichick later surpassed in five seasons.

22. A. Alabama. Late September 1968 saw the Red Sox still using Fenway Park, so the Patriots played their "home" opener at Legion Field in Birmingham. The Pats were blown out by Alabama alum Joe Namath and the Jets, 47-31.

23. C. Gino Cappelletti. The kicker-wide receiver and all-time leading scorer in American Football League history didn't beat out receivers Troy Brown, Irving Fryar, Stanley Morgan, or kicker Tom Vinatieri for the all-time team, but the Pats found a spot to honor classy Cappy.

24. D. Tennessee Titans. In a frigid 4-degree 2003 night playoff game, the Pats beat the Titans, 17-14. In a freak October 18, 2009 snowstorm, the Pats rolled up a 45-0 halftime lead over Tennessee on their way to winning by a club-record 59 points.

25. Eight straight weeks. The Pats scored 39, 31, 45, 45, 36, 31, 34 and 38 while beating every team in their division, as well as Indianapolis, Detroit and Chicago, plus Pittsburgh and Green Bay, who would play each other in the Super Bowl.

26. Matt Cassel. And he did pretty well, throwing for 3,693 yards and 21 touchdowns while helping New England to an 11-5 record. The Patriots just missed the playoffs, however, and

Cassel was traded to the Chiefs the following year with Mike Vrabel for a second-round draft pick.

27. Jim Plunkett out of Stanford (1971) and Drew Bledsoe from Washington State (1993) are the only number-one QBs taken by the Pats, through 2011.

28. D. John Stephens. The running back out of Northwestern State (Louisiana) ran for 1,168 yards as a rookie in 1988, earning a Pro Bowl berth. He was displaced at running back in 1991 by 1991 AP Rookie of the Year Leonard Russell.

29. False. Future Hall of Fame cornerback Mike Haynes was awarded Defensive Rookie of the Year in 1976. Haynes was the only Patriot so honored before Mayo.

30. B. South Dakota State. He left the Jackrabbits as the school's all-time leading scorer when SDSU was still a Division II school. He played football in Amsterdam in the World League of American Football before signing with the Patriots in 1996.

31. C. 21 games. From October 5, 2003 to October 31, 2004, the Patriots had the longest winning streak in NFL history.

32. A. Buffalo Bills. Drew Bledsoe and the Bills blanked the Patriots at Rich Stadium, 31-0, to open the 2003 season. Fittingly, that 14-2 season ended with the Pats blanking Buffalo in Foxboro by that same 31-0 score.

33. B. 7-2. The Pats purposely took a safety late in the game by snapping the ball through the end zone because they were pinned deep in their own territory on a day with 15-degree wind chill. The Pats won the battle of teams that entered the game at 1-11.

34. D. Andre Tippett. He scooped up 19 fumbles in his 11-year Hall of Fame career, breaking the mark of 16 set by former teammate Steve Nelson, the first Patriot with three recoveries in a game. Bob Dee recovered five for the 1961 season.

35. Baseball. Gostkowski was All-State in Mississippi in football, soccer and baseball, pitching Madison Central High to the 2002 state title. He was All-Conference USA in both baseball and football at Memphis.

36. Dan Gronkowski, like older brother Rob, plays tight end; he joined the Patriots in 2011. Chris Gronkowski plays running back, appearing with both Dallas and Indianapolis.

37. C: 3. Troy Brown picked off three passes as a cornerback for the Patriots, placing him second on the team behind Eugene Wilson's four. Brown also returned 12 punts, caught 17 passes, and scored a touchdown in 2004.

38. Three. The Pats lost 6-3 to the Jets in 1991, 6-0 to the Colts in 1992 and 6-0 to the Jets in 1993. Blech!

39. False. The 2007 Patriots actually lost their first two preseason games, both by a field goal, to Tampa Bay and Tennessee. The Pats finished the preseason by beating the Panthers and the Giants, one of three times they met the Giants that season.

40. B. Oakland Raiders. The Pats sent a fourth-round pick to the Raiders for the troubled wide receiver, who responded to his new environment with an NFL-best 23 touchdown catches. In 2010 the Pats traded Moss back to his original team, the Vikings.

41. True. Laurence Maroney led the Patriots with 835 yards rushing in 2007.

42. Randy Moss scored one more point than Stephen Gostkowski, 138-137. Moss scored 23 touchdowns, while Gostkowski kicked 74 extra points and 21 field goals in 2007. They finished second and third in the NFL to Packers kicker Mason Crosby (141 points).

43. True. Before sudden death overtime became the rule, the Pats had nine ties, but the last was in 1967. Since the institution of regular season overtime in 1974, the Pats have not had to kiss their sister.

44. C. 4. Subbing at quarterback for injured Tom Brady, Matt Cassel and the Pats hit 40 points against the Broncos, 41-7, the Dolphins, 48-28, the Raiders, 49-26 and the eventual NFC champion Cardinals in a Foxboro snowstorm, 47-7. The 11-5 Pats missed the playoffs on tiebreakers.

45. True. The Patriots had beaten the Jets twice previously before falling to New York in Foxboro by a 28-21 score in 2010.

46. Dick MacPherson. He came from Syracuse University to coach the Patriots in 1991 and 1992. He was replaced by Bill Parcells, who left New England for the Jets and was replaced by ex-Jets coach Pete Carroll, who was later replaced by Bill Belichick, a Jets assistant who replaced Parcells as head coach in New York for one day.

47. A. Baltimore Colts. At age 23, Bill Belichick was a $25-per-week special assistant in 1975 for Ted Marchibroda and his hometown Baltimore Colts. Belichick moved up the pay scale and worked in Detroit as a receivers coach before switching to special teams and defense.

48. A. 5. The Pats were 5-11 in 2000, Bill Belichick's first season as a head coach since 1995. The 2001 Patriots reversed the previous year's record and won their first Super Bowl.

49. Tackle Nate Solder was taken by the Patriots with the 17th overall pick in 2011. The 6-foot-8 Denver native began his college career at Colorado as a tight end.

50. B. Corey Dillon. Dillon rushed for 1,635 yards in 2004, breaking Curtis Martin's 1995 record of 1,487.

51. C. Stanley Morgan. His 10,352 career receiving yards are likewise the most in franchise history.

52. Tony Franklin. Franklin, who kicked 64- and 65-yard field goals at Texas A&M, had plenty of, um, foot. After six seasons with the Eagles, he joined the Patriots in 1984 and spent four years with New England, making the Pro Bowl after the 1986 season.

53. C. Hall of Fame linebacker Andre Tippett had exactly 100 sacks.

54. D. Romania. Eight years after his family survived the Communist Revolution of 1989, the Meskos won a green card through a visa lottery program. Zoltan discovered football when his kick broke a ceiling fixture during gym class in Ohio. His teacher said he could either pay for the fixture or play football…. Good choice.

55. New York Giants. The Pats beat the Giants, 17-6, on October 12, 2003. The Red Sox were rained out that evening, and the following night the Sox embarked on their curse-crushing baseball comeback against New York.

56. 2003. The Patriots beat the Houston Texans at Reliant Stadium in Houston in overtime on November 23. Foreshadowing their Super Bowl victory against Carolina, the game against Houston was won by an Adam Vinatieri field goal on the final play.

57. Three. The Pats blanked the Cowboys and Dolphins by the same 12-0 score in a four-week span and ended the season with a 31-0 shutout of Buffalo.

58. A. 8. His interception percentage of 1.4 was among the top 20 in history, though it wasn't a career mark. His 0.8 percentage in 2010 was second in NFL history.

59. B. Tony Eason. Eason was brought down 59 times in 1984, an NFL record for one year until the 60 barrier was shattered by Jet Ken O'Brien and Cardinal Neil Lomax in 1985. Randall Cunningham of the Eagles broke the 70 barrier in 1986 and David Carr set the standard as a first-year Texan with 76 in 2002.

60. C. 9. The Patriots went from 1966 (8-4-2) to 1976 (11-3) without a winning season in between.

61. A. Drew Bledsoe. Bledsoe attempted 691 passes in 1994 for the New England Patriots.

62. Cardinals and Titans and Bears, oh my! Arizona (47-7 in 2008), Tennessee (59-0 in 2009) and Chicago (36-7 in 2010) were all snowed under in Foxboro.

63. Drew Bledsoe (29,657), his Pats predecessor.

64. C. Andre Tippett. The Hall of Fame linebacker recovered 19 fumbles, as many as Tom Brady had, through 2011. Quarterbacks Steve Grogan (34) and Drew Bledsoe (27) had the most fumble recoveries in team history, but defenders Willie McGinest (15), Mike Haynes (11) and Vince Wilfork (8) were among the leaders in piling up turnovers.

65. False. The Pats finished 5-11 in 2000, Drew Bledsoe's last year as the starter.

66. B. 2. Through 2011, the lowest rushing total the Patriots have held an opponent to is 2 yards rushing in a 41-0 blowout of the Chargers on December 17, 1961.

67. San Diego Chargers, Miami Dolphins, Green Bay Packers and Denver Broncos. The Pats did not win from September 22 to November 5. The defending Super Bowl champs went 9-7 and missed the playoffs, but the Pats ruined Miami's postseason hopes in the season finale.

68. C. 20. Before the 24-20 loss to the Giants in the closing minute on November 6, 2011, the last time the Pats lost at home

during the regular season was a 33-10 defeat by the Steelers on November 30, 2008.

69. D. 74. The 16-0 Pats of 2007 set a record for most touchdowns and Stephen Gostkowski was good on all 74 of them.

70. B. Irving Fryar. The Heisman Trophy voters thought Fryar the third-best player on Nebraska's 1983 powerhouse club, with running back Mike Rozier winning the Heisman and quarterback Turner Gill named a finalist. But Fryar was the outstanding pro, spending nine seasons in New England, recording 5,726 yards, and helping the Pats reach the Super Bowl for the first time.

71. A. 5. Only once in 2002-03 did Tedy Bruschi intercept a pass and not take it in for a touchdown. He ran back interceptions for TDs of 48 yards (in Oakland) and 27 yards on Thanksgiving (in Detroit). His next two picks in 2003 went for touchdowns (against Philadelphia and Miami) before picking off a pass and not taking it to paydirt, though it helped secure a win over the Jets.

72. Pete Carroll. He was fired after finishing 8 8 in 1999, the only one of Carroll's three years in New England that the Pats did not make the playoffs.

73. D. Rod Rust lasted one year on the job.

74. Hartford, Connecticut. Bob Kraft had a deal in 1998 to move the Patriots to Connecticut before problems with the property, along with incentives from Massachusetts, led the team right back to Foxboro. Kraft also considered Rhode Island.

75. Pete Carroll. After losing the Super Bowl to Green Bay, Bill Parcells left to join the New York Jets in 1997.

76. D. New York Jets. The Pats beat them in the AFC Wild Card game at the Meadowlands, 22-14. The Pats defeated Buffalo in an AFL playoff game in 1963, necessitated by a tie at the end of the regular season.

77. B. Miami Dolphins. The Pats won the 1985 AFC Championship game in Miami, 31-14, ending an 18-game losing streak at the Orange Bowl that dated to 1966.

78. C. 1991. Foxboro hosted its first game on natural grass 20 years after it opened.

79. C. Raymond Clayborn. The Pats cornerback appeared in 161 straight games, from his rookie year in 1977—when the

schedule was 14 games—until injury forced him out in 1987. He had passed Gino Cappelletti's record of 152 at the start of the '87 season.

80. C. John Hannah. The legendary guard was the lone inductee in the first Patriots Hall of Fame class in 1991, the same year he was inducted into the Pro Football Hall of Fame. Steve Grogan (1995), Bruce Armstrong (2001), Stanley Morgan (2007) and more than a dozen others have joined Hannah in the Pats Hall of Fame.

81. True. Drew Bledsoe, the first overall pick by the Pats in the 1993 draft and first in numerous franchise records until Tom Brady took his spot, was elected to the Patriots Hall of Fame at Gillette Stadium in 2011.

82. Danny Woodhead. Woodhead, out of Division II Chadron State in Nebraska, rushed 97 times for 551 yards for the 2010 Pats, a 5.68 yards-per-carry average to set the club record for 90 carries or more. Don Calhoun had held the mark with 5.59 yards (721 yards on 129 rushes) since 1976.

83. True. Welker caught an NFL-best 112 passes in 2007 after coming to the Pats from the Dolphins for two draft picks. A great runner and kicker in high school, he was deemed too small and only received a scholarship to Texas Tech because another player backed out. Undrafted, he was picked up by Miami after San Diego cut him.

84. D. 587. The Patriots broke the scoring mark of 566 set by the 1998 Minnesota Vikings. The record was erased on the same play that Randy Moss established a new record for touchdown catches, with his 23rd of the year on a 65-yard bomb from Tom Brady in the final game of the regular season against the Giants.

85. A. 10. The Pats had just five interceptions (tying an NFL record) along with five fumbles in 2010. The closest team to New England's TO mark was the 1982 Kansas City Chiefs, who had 12 during strike-shortened 1982.

86. Providence. It is 21 miles from the stadium to the Rhode Island capital and 33 miles to the Massachusetts capital.

87. D. Andre Tippett. Though he became a Hall of Famer—like teammate Mike Haynes—Tippett had the misfortune of debuting in the truncated 1982 strike season and did not record a sack. The linebacker appeared in five straight Pro Bowls starting in 1984.

88. C. Steve Grogan. Before Tom Brady's league-leading 28 touchdown passes in 2002, Grogan threw the same number of TDs to tie Cleveland's Brian Sipe for the NFL lead in 1979.

89. B. Raymond Berry. Berry never lost an opener in his five-plus seasons with the Pats (1984-89).

90. C. Babe Parilli. Drew Bledsoe's 27 interceptions in 1994 tied the Babe's 1964 mark.

91. D. San Diego Chargers. After making the remarks in Miami after the season opening win, Tom Brady threw for 423 yards in a 35-21 victory in the home opener, with the Chargers turning the ball over four times.

92. B. 8,446. Raiders fans didn't "travel" in 1960. The first Boston meeting of the teams in the inaugural AFL season didn't draw many fans. The Pats did beat Oakland, 34-28, to start the club's first-ever winning streak. The home finale against Houston brought out the year's biggest crowd, 27,123.

93. C. 1995. The Patriots sold out in April following their first playoff appearance since 1986.

94. True. Through 2011, New England's four Thanksgiving games had all been on the road: a 20-17 loss in Dallas in 1984, a 34-9 turkey against the Lions in 2000, a 20-12 win in Detroit in 2002, and a 45-24 Lion taming in 2010.

95. A. Joe Kapp. Despite leading the Minnesota Vikings to the 1969 NFL title, Kapp was not tendered a job after losing Super Bowl IV to Kansas City. Commissioner Pete Rozelle interfered with Kapp's signing with the Patriots, resulting in a later lawsuit. Kapp was 1-9 as a starter in a 2-12 Pats season.

96. D. Adam Vinatieri. He nailed a 57-yard kick on November 11, 2002 in Chicago, breaking the mark of 55 yards shared by Vinatieri (1998) and Matt Bahr (1995).

97. Wes Welker. On October 10, 2004, at Foxboro, Welker stepped in for Miami's injured kicker and recorded the first four points of his NFL career… with his foot. Though he was busy all day, the future Pro Bowl wide receiver did not catch a pass as the Pats won, 24-10.

98. D. Ty Law. Six of his 36 career interceptions, tied for most in club history with Raymond Clayborn, were returned for touchdowns. Tedy Bruschi had four, but Hall of Famer Mike Haynes returned just one of his 28 Pats picks for a touchdown.

99. C. Kansas City Chiefs. The Patriots have yet to face the Chiefs in the playoffs, nor did they play the Dallas Texans in the AFL postseason before they relocated to K.C. in 1963.

100. Head coach Raymond Berry's last year was 1989, Rod Rust lasted the 1990 season, Dick MacPherson coached in 1991-92, and then Bill Parcells took over in 1993.

101. B. Tom Landry. The iconic Dallas coach won 20 times in the playoffs, lost 16, including twice to Pittsburgh's Chuck Noll (16-8). Vince Lombardi (9-1) coached when there were far fewer playoff games. Bill Belichick won 17 of his first 24 playoff games, including a 1-1 mark with the 1994 Browns.

102. Four. Bill Belichick's Pats went 14-2 in 2003, 2004 and 2011, and had a 16-0 regular season in 2007.

103. A. Billy Cundiff. A Pro Bowl kicker the previous year, Cundiff lined up for a 32-yard, game-tying field goal try in the closing seconds to send the AFC Championship Game into overtime. He was wide left—as opposed to Scott Norwood's infamous wide right for the Bills 20 years earlier. Matt Stover was the Ravens' all-time leading scorer, and Jim O'Brien's last-second, 32-yard kick won Super Bowl V for the Baltimore Colts.

104. Kyle Arrington. Though some thought he might be released in training camp, the third-year corner from Hofstra not only made the Pats but thrived in the banged-up secondary. Seven interceptions tied Green Bay's Charles Woodson and San Diego's Eric Weddle for tops in the NFL.

105. B. Andre Carter. Arriving in New England with far less hype than former Redskins teammate/malcontent Albert Haynesworth, Carter had 4.5 sacks on November 13, 2011, taking down Jets QB Mark Sanchez on successive plays in the fourth quarter of a 37-16 win. Carter tied with Mark Anderson for the team lead with 10 sacks each.

106. Vince Wilfork. The 30-year-old defensive tackle enjoyed his fourth Pro Bowl season in 2011, establishing career highs for sacks (3.5), passes defended (3), and, of course, interceptions. His first INT came against the Chargers, rumbling for 28 yards. Two weeks later he picked off an Oakland pass. In Washington he scored for the first time, falling on a fumble in the end zone in a game the Pats won by a touchdown.

107. False. Steve Grogan was sacked in the end zone for a safety late in the 46-10 rout by the Bears in Super Bowl XX. On New

England's first play from scrimmage in Super Bowl XLVI, Tom Brady was called for intentional grounding in the end zone, resulting in a safety for the first points of the game for the Giants.

108. C. 5. The only returning defensive starter for New England at the same position during the four-year interval was nose tackle Vince Wilfork. On offense there was continuity at left tackle (Matt Light) and left guard (Logan Mankins), at wide receiver (Wes Welker) and, of course, at quarterback (Tom Brady).

109. B. Indianapolis. Super Bowl XLVI took place at Lucas Oil Stadium in Indianapolis.

110. C. 16. Tom Brady completed 16 consecutive passes during Super Bowl XLVI, breaking the mark of 13 in a row by San Francisco's Joe Montana in Super Bowl XXIV. Brady's streak ended after Aaron Hernandez's touchdown grab put the Patriots up in the third quarter, 17-9. Unfortunately, the end of the game is better remembered for balls not caught by Pats receivers.

The Brady Bunch (of Questions)

1. D. 1,327. Tom Brady broke the mark of 1,257 yards in three games set by Drew Brees in 2006, and he also surpassed Curt Warner's 1,221 in 2001. Brady threw for 1,277 yards in five Super Bowl starts.

2. Sixth round, out of Michigan

3. B. David Nugent. With no first-round pick as compensation for Bill Belichick leaving the Jets, the Patriots chose Hawaii tackle Adrian Klemm (second round), ASU running back J.R. Redmond (third round), and Boise State tight end Dave Stachleski (fifth round) ahead of Tom Brady of Michigan in the sixth round (199th overall). Nugent, a Purdue defensive end, was taken two spots after Brady with the 201st pick.

4. C. 300. Tom Brady averaged 300.4 yards per game, or 4,806 yards during the 16-0 season.

5. 2009. Tom Brady was lost for 2008 with ligament damage in his left knee in the first game of the season. He returned the next year to throw for 4,398 yards and 28 touchdowns to earn AP Comeback Player of the Year honors.

6. Catcher. Les Expos chose Tom Brady in the 18th round of the 1995 draft. He passed and went to Michigan.

7. Miami Dolphins. Tom Brady threw for six scores and accrued a perfect rating of 158.3 in the 49-28 win over Miami on October 21, 2007.

8. C. Mo Lewis. The New York Jets linebacker sent Drew Bledsoe, who had signed to a 10-year contract with the Patriots in the offseason, to the hospital. The Jets won the September 23 game, 10-3, but New England was introduced to its new franchise quarterback. NFL Films called it *The Hit That Changed History*.

9. B. Indianapolis Colts. Tom Brady beat Peyton Manning and the Colts, 44-13, in his first NFL start on September 30, 2001.

Your Father's Patriots

1. Guard John Hannah and defensive back Mike Haynes were on the All-1980s first team. Andre Tippett was on the second team defense.

2. D. Oakland Raiders. So many penalties went against New England, it became known as the "Ben Dreith Game," for the ref's name. The most damaging call was roughing quarterback Ken Stabler on third-and-18 in the final minute. Stabler ran for the winning score with 10 seconds left, and Oakland went on to win the Super Bowl.

3. False. The Pats won the 1983 season opener at home against the Colts, but they lost the rematch in Baltimore in October. The Houston Oilers, who would relocate a decade later, opposed the Colts in their last game in Baltimore in December. The Pats put a 50-spot on the Colts the first time they met in Indianapolis in 1984.

4. C. Kansas State. A Kansas high school star in basketball, track and, of course, football, Steve Grogan displayed a powerful arm and remarkable agility. After leading K-State to the Sun Bowl as a senior, the Patriots took him in the fifth round with the 116th overall pick in 1975. He would spend his entire 15-year career in New England.

5. A. Baltimore Colts. The Pats lost three times to new division rival Baltimore before finally winning the last game of 1971, year two of the merger. In between the Pats lost to NFL, now NFC teams: the Giants, Cardinals, Vikings, Lions, Cowboys, 49ers and the Browns, who, like the Colts, were an old-line NFL team relocated to the AFC.

6. B. 1973. Future Hall of Famer John Hannah was chosen fourth overall out of Alabama, Sam "Bam" Cunningham was taken 11th overall from USC, and Purdue's Darryl Stingley was the 19th pick in the country.

7. Jim Plunkett. The reigning Heisman Trophy winner and first overall draft pick, Plunkett christened the new stadium in Foxboro, called Schaefer Stadium, with a 20-6 win over the Oakland Raiders.

8. Jack Tatum. The Oakland safety, nicknamed "The Assassin," collided with Darryl Stingley in an August 12, 1978, pre-season game. Stingley's head hit Tatum's shoulder pad, severely damaging his spinal cord. Stingley never walked again. Tatum never contacted him, though Stingley forgave Tatum before his death in 2007.

9. C. San Francisco 49ers. The Pats received backup QB Tom Owens, plus two first-round picks in 1976 that the Patriots used for center Pete Brock and safety Tim Fox, and a 1977 second-round pick used for running back Horace Ivory. The Patriots were fine at QB with Steve Grogan, but Plunkett went on to greatness later as a Raider.

10. True. In a classic mismatch, the 11-2 Pats faced the 0-13 Bucs in the last game of the year in Tampa Bay. The playoff-bound Pats won their sixth straight game and handed the Bucs their 14th straight defeat and a place in the record books, 31-14. It was also Tampa Bay's last game as an AFC team before swapping conferences with Seattle.

11. John Smith. An emergency ground rule allowed the officials to have the grounds crew clear the yard lines with a snowplow. When the plow operator got to the middle of the field, he veered to the 23-yard line, the exact spot where the holder would set up the field goal attempt. Despite Miami's protests, the kick was good for the game's only points. New England's 3-0 win helped the Pats reach the playoffs, where they were trounced in—you guessed it—Miami.

12. B. Colorado. The Pats were quickly bounced from the 1978 playoffs and Chuck Fairbanks made a hash of things in Boulder, where he went 7-26. He had come to the Patriots from Oklahoma, where the university had to forfeit nine games and could not appear in bowl games for two years because of recruiting violations.

13. Sam "Bam" Cunningham, with 5,453 yards. He spent his entire career as a Pat between 1973 and 1982.

14. Harold Jackson (1,013 yards) and Stanley Morgan (1,002)

15. Raymond Clayborn. The durable cornerback out of Texas spent 13 seasons with the Patriots and still owns a share of the franchise interception record with Ty Law with 36 INTs.

16. C. Remington Razors. Victor Kiam's wife gave him a razor as a gift and, using the catchphrase he made famous in commercials, "I liked it so much I bought the company." But Kiam sold the Patriots in 1991.

17. D. 8. In one year the Patriots flipped records from 3-11 to 11-3 and earned the AFC East title.

18. C. 1971. The Patriots played their first game as the New England Patriots in 1971 after relocating from Harvard to Foxboro.

19. Bay State Patriots. The name was rejected because it would have been too easy to call them the B.S. Patriots, especially during the team's down years in the early 1970s.

20. D. 3,165 yards. Even more impressive was the fact that no Patriot reached 800 yards. Sam "Bam" Cunningham led the run-at-will Pats with 768 rushing yards, followed by Horace Ivory (693), Andy Johnson (675), Steve Grogan (539) and Don Calhoun (391). The 11-5 Patriots reached the playoffs for the second time in three years.

The Super Bowl Challenge

1. Tony Eason in Super Bowl XX against the Bears. It did not go well.

2. B. Tony Franklin. The barefoot kicker knocked a 36-yarder through the uprights to give the Patriots an early lead in Super Bowl XX against the Bears. Chicago scored the game's next 44 points.

3. C. 4. Through 2012, the other Super Bowl rematches besides Giants and Patriots are Dolphins-Redskins, 49ers-Bengals, Cowboys-Bills, and Steelers-Cowboys (three times).

4. D. Ken Walter. The Pats punter put the ball down for the last-second kicks that won Super Bowl XXXVI and XXXVIII. He also was the holder in the snowy conditions during the fabled "tuck rule" playoff game in the snow against Oakland. He was actually cut late in the 2003 season in favor of Brooks

Barnard, but Walter later got his job back and was in place for the Super Bowl against Carolina.

5. Deion Branch. He tied a Super Bowl record with 11 catches and was named MVP in the victory over the Eagles after spending all day thanking his coaches from Monroe High (Albany, GA), Jones County JC (Ellisville, MS) and Louisville.

6. New Orleans and the Superdome. The Pats lost in Super Bowl XIX and XXXII in New Orleans prior to their last-second upset of the Rams at the Superdome in Super Bowl XXXVI.

7. B. Jacksonville. The Patriots pulled out a 24-21 victory over the Eagles at All Tell Stadium in Super Bowl XXXIX. Like the previous two Patriots Super Bowl victories in New Orleans and Houston, this one was also decided by a field goal margin.

8. B. Rodney Harrison. He picked off two Donovan McNab passes, including his final throw with nine seconds left to ensure a third Super Bowl title for the Patriots. Tedy Bruschi had an interception and Asante Samuel a fumble recovery in Super Bowl XXXIX.

9. D. Tampa Bay Buccaneers. The Bucs won Super Bowl XXXVII over Oakland in the one season in four that did not end in a Patriotic celebration.

Your Grandfather's Patriots

1. B. The Foolish Club. The National Football League had rebuffed some of the owners from purchasing NFL teams, so they formed their own league at considerable expense with little guarantee they'd ever make a dime. The fools win.

2. C. $4.75. It wasn't a bad investment, either. When Billy Sullivan bought out all available shares of stock in 1970, he paid $25 per share.

3. D. Jim Colclough. The running back out of Boston College, by way of Medford, caught a 10-yard touchdown pass from Butch Songin on September 9, 1960.

4. C. Gino Cappelletti did it all. Not only was he a great receiver in the pass-happy AFL, he was also a defensive back, kick returner and kicker, booting 176 field goals and 342 PATs for the Pats.

5. C. 45. Jim Nance ran for 11 of those TDs in 1966.

6. D. The San Diego Chargers. In 1963, after tying the Bills for first in the division at 7-6-1, the Pats won a playoff in Buffalo. The Pats went to San Diego for the title game and were routed, 51-10.

7. John F. Kennedy. The new president, who hadn't progressed past the junior varsity team at Harvard in the 1930s because of injury and illness, kept his day job. The Kennedys still liked to play a lot of touch football, however.

8. D. UMass-Amherst. The Patriots trained there for two years and later returned (1969-1975). The Pats also trained at Phillips Academy (1962-1968), Bryant (1976-2002) and Gillette Stadium (since 2003).

9. D. A tricornered hat from Revolutionary War days. Beneath the hat was the player's number. The following year came the iconic Patriot hiking a ball.

10. D. New York Titans. The Titans, forerunners to the Jets, were beaten by the Boston Patriots, 28-24, on September 17, 1960 eight days after the Pats debuted with a loss to Denver.

11. Three. The AFL trio: kicker-wide receiver Gino Cappelletti (#20), defensive tackle Jim Hunt (#79) and defensive end Bob Dee (#89).

12. Gino Cappelletti and Jim Nance. Cappy was the team's kicker and top receiver, recording an AFL-record 155 points in 1964. Jim Nance likewise set an AFL record with his 1,458 yards while picking up the MVP in 1966.

13. 1-D, 2-B, 3-A, 4-C, or 1-Nickerson, 2-Fenway, 3-Alumni, 4-Harvard.

14. C. The Red Sox were never the basis of an NFL team's name, though the Braves were (the name changed to Redskins when the club moved to Fenway Park in 1933 and subsequently relocated to Washington). The Yanks played at Fenway from 1944-48 before relocating to New York… and taking the name Bulldogs.

15. They got shut out first. Buffalo whitewashed the Patriots in Boston, 13-0, on September 23, 1960. With a week off to think about it—and practice—the Pats went to Los Angeles and blanked the Chargers, 35-0.

16. The Pats won. The Dolphins made a game of it, though. Down 20-0 in the third quarter at the Orange Bowl, Miami scored

two touchdowns behind Dick Wood (his real name). The Patriots held on for the 20-14 win.

17. C. New York Jets. Second-year quarterback Joe Namath helped the Jets beat the Pats at Shea Stadium, 38-28, despite Babe Parilli's 379 yards passing. The Pats and Jets had tied earlier in the year, and that half-game made all the difference. The Bills won their final game to claim the East title, but Buffalo lost to Kansas City for the AFL title and a spot in Super Bowl I.

18. B. Phil Bissell. Given the assignment to draw what Boston's new football logo should be, Bissell nailed it and Pat was born. All he got was $100 from Patriots owner Billy Sullivan, so he might as well get credit here.

19. False. Gino Cappelletti kicked just one field goal at the University of Minnesota. He was the quarterback at Minnesota—and did a little kicking—but had to go to Canada to find gridiron work. The AFL gave him the chance to return stateside.

20. Bob Gallagher and Fred Cusick. Gallagher, a former semi-pro basketball player who attended Boston College, was also the first Dolphins announcer. Cusick was color commentator, but he was much better known for his 45 years calling Bruins hockey.

Pats Firsts

1. B. Denver Broncos. The Broncos won the Friday night game at Boston University's Nickerson Field, 13-10.

2. D. Butch Songin. He started 12 games under center for the fledgling 1960 Patriots.

3. C. 1977. They were the second-to-last AFC East team to adopt cheerleaders. The Jets remained cheer-free until 2006.

4. John Hannah. He was inducted into the Hall of Fame in 1991. Hannah was All-Pro his last 10 years in the NFL. He was named a guard on the NFL's 1970s and 1980s teams as well as its 75th anniversary team.

5. D. Tampa Bay Buccaneers. The Pats stomped the Bucs in front of 84,000 at London's Wembley Stadium, 35-7.

6. C. Tampa Bay Buccaneers. Jason Staurovsky's 27-yard field goal 3:08 into overtime on December 11, 1988, provided a 10-7 win in Tampa. That put an end to a 10-game OT losing streak,

including two losses apiece to Miami and Pittsburgh, that dated to the adoption of regular-season overtime in 1974.

7. D. Jim Nance. The second-year back blasted through the 1,000-yard barrier with 1,458 yards in 1966, a club record that stood until 1995. Nance gained 1,000 yards in 1967, too.

8. A. Ron Burton. He rushed for 127 yards on 16 carries in Denver on October 23, 1960, the first game in which the Patriots surpassed 200 yards passing or 200 yards rushing as a team. No matter, the Pats blew a 24-point lead and lost, 31-24.

The Red Sox

5

Red Sox Basics

1. As of 2011, a Red Sox outfielder was the last major leaguer to record 40 home runs and 15 triples in the same year. Who is he?

2. Which Red Sox slugger was the first player in history to hit 40 or more home runs for two different teams?
   A. Jimmie Foxx
   B. Jackie Jensen
   C. Manny Ramirez
   D. Babe Ruth

3. What one-time member of the Red Sox holds the all-time record for 40-homer seasons with 11 but never had a 40-homer season during his time with the Red Sox?

4. What year did the Red Sox and Yankees first meet in the postseason?
   A. 1978
   B. 1999
   C. 2003
   D. 2004

5. Which member of the Red Sox played his final major league game in the 1978 one-game playoff against the Yankees at Fenway Park?
   A. Bob Bailey
   B. Jack Brohamer
   C. Dick Drago
   D. George Scott

6. True or false? In Boston's first 110 years as a major league club, Jacoby Ellsbury was the only player to lead the American League in steals and triples in the same season.

7. Through 2011, the Red Sox had three players hit 40 home runs and fan less than 75 times in a season. Which of the following did *not* pull off that feat?
   A. Rico Petrocelli
   B. Jim Rice
   C. Ted Williams
   D. Carl Yastrzemski

8. Whose club record for home runs in a season did David Ortiz break in 2006?

9. Ted Williams batted .344 over his career, the best mark of any Red Sox hitter. Name the two Hall of Famers who accrued at least 1,500 career at bats with the Sox and came within 10 points of the Splendid Splinter's club batting figure.

10. Three players have hit career home run number 500 in a Red Sox uniform. Name them.

11. During the second inning of a 2007 game at Yankee Stadium, Terry Francona was told by an MLB official to go into the dugout runway and do what?

    A. Empty his pockets to see if he was carrying a file to deface the ball.
    B. Read a few lines for an MLB commercial.
    C. Show them he was wearing a uniform.
    D. Urinate in a cup.

12. Who owned the Red Sox career saves record before Jonathon Papelbon broke it in 2009?

13. Which boastful Yankees slugger said of a late-inning home run at Fenway, "It was an insurance run, so I hit it to the Prudential Building"?

A. Yogi Berra

B. Reggie Jackson

C. Mickey Mantle

D. Alex Rodriguez

14. With Jon Lester's no-hitter in 2008, Jason Varitek set a record for most no-hitters caught. How many for Tek?

15. Which Red Sox manager was the last to win a World Series before Terry Francona?

A. Jack Barry

B. Ed Barrow

C. Bill Carrigan

D. Joe Cronin

16. Which Red Sox manager was the last to win *two* World Series before Terry Francona?

A. Jack Barry

B. Ed Barrow

C. Bill Carrigan

D. Joe Cronin

17. Through 2011, two Red Sox managers had been named Manager of the Year. Jimy Williams was one, who was the other?

    A. Terry Francona

    B. Darrell Johnson

    C. John McNamara

    D. Dick Williams

18. Florida is one of the 10 states where the Red Sox have held spring training since 1901. Name six other states that have served as spring sites for the Sox.

19. Of the four full-season managers who preceded Terry Francona, which won the most postseason games?

    A. Butch Hobson

    B. Kevin Kennedy

    C. Grady Little

    D. Jimy Williams

20. Which Red Sox pitcher ended the team's 13-game postseason losing streak that began in 1986?

    A. Tom Gordon

    B. Pedro Martinez

    C. Pete Schourek

D. Tim Wakefield

21. What is the ground rule for a ball that gets stuck in the ladder above the Green Monster at Fenway Park?

22. What future Red Sox infielder started two triple plays in one game against Boston?
A. George Burns
B. Gary Gaetti
C. Carney Lansford
D. Bill Mueller

23. Who played the Red Sox-obsessed fan in the 2005 U.S. film *Fever Pitch*?

24. Why did the Farrelly brothers have to re-shoot the ending to the 2005 U.S. film *Fever Pitch*?

25. On June 27, 2003, the Red Sox set a record for the most runs scored before an out was recorded in a major league game. How many Sox touched home before out number one?
A. 10
B. 11
C. 14
D. 25

26. Stephen King wrote a horror novel using a real Red Sox pitcher's name. Who was the hurler?

27. Who was the first Red Sox pitcher to claim the Cy Young Award?

28. Whose 55 career pinch hits are the club record?
    A. Joe Cronin
    B. Dalton Jones
    C. Rick Miller
    D. Jason Varitek

29. Who was the first Red Sox catcher to hit .300 while catching 100 games in a season?
    A. Rick Ferrell
    B. Carlton Fisk
    C. Wally Schang
    D. Jason Varitek

30. Through 2011, who holds Boston's all-time stolen base mark with an even 300?
    A. Rick Burleson
    B. Jacoby Ellsbury
    C. Tommy Harper
    D. Harry Hooper

31. True or false? Jacoby Ellsbury was the first player in Red Sox history to lead the league in steals

multiple times.

32. Pedro Martinez won the 1997 National League Cy Young Award a week before being traded to the Red Sox. How many Cy Youngs did Pedro win in Boston?

33. With Montreal unable to meet his salary demands, the Red Sox acquired Pedro Martinez in November 1997 for two top minor league hurlers: one the son of a former Sox slugger and the other a New England-born hurler. Name them.

34. Who was the first Red Sox switch-hitter to homer from each side of the plate in the same game?
    A. Luis Alicea
    B. Bill Mueller
    C. Reggie Smith
    D. Jason Varitek

35. The Red Sox have the only player in baseball history to hit grand slams from each side of the plate in one game. Who was he?
    A. Luis Alicea
    B. Bill Mueller
    C. Reggie Smith
    D. Jason Varitek

36. Who won more batting titles, Ted Williams or Wade Boggs?

37. Who was the first Red Sox player to homer in his first major league at bat?
    A. Ted Cox
    B. Bill LeFebvre
    C. Fred Lynn
    D. Ted Williams

38. Jacoby Ellsbury's breakout 32-homer season in 2011 represented an increase in how many home runs over 2010?
    A. 8
    B. 16
    C. 24
    D. 32

39. Who owns the Red Sox record for most saves in a season?
    A. Tom Gordon
    B. Derek Lowe
    C. Jonathon Papelbon
    D. Bob Stanley

40. Who pitched more complete games for the Red Sox, Roger Clemens or Babe Ruth?

41. Did the 2011 Red Sox have a worse winning percentage for the first 12 games of the year or the last dozen?

42. True or false? Bobby Valentine is the first manager in Red Sox history who also managed the New York Mets.

43. With the appointment of Bobby Valentine, how many men have managed the Red Sox?
    A. 35
    B. 40
    C. 45
    D. 50

44. How many Red Sox managers have later been inducted in the Hall of Fame?
    A. 5
    B. 7
    C. 9
    D. 11

45. Who had at least 200 hits and 100 walks in four consecutive seasons with the Red Sox?
    A. Wade Boggs
    B. Nomar Garciaparra
    C. Tris Speaker
    D. Ted Williams

46. Red Sox hitters won four batting titles in a five-year span that ended in 2003. Name the three Sox who claimed those batting crowns.

47. Which two Red Sox pitchers won the pitching Triple Crown for leading the league in wins, ERA, and strikeouts in a season?

48. Five pitchers who spent part of their career with the Red Sox reached 3,000 career strikeouts before walking 1,000 batters. Name four of them.

49. In their 110 years as a franchise, who is the only Red Sox player with 30 homers and 30 steals in the same year?

50. Who hit the longest home run at Fenway Park, now marked by a red seat?

51. Who is the only Red Sox pitcher to log 3,000 innings with the club?

52. Which Hall of Famer is the only Red Sox pitcher to lose 20 games more than once?

A. Dennis Eckersley

B. Lefty Grove

C. Red Ruffing

D. Cy Young

53. Who was re-acquired by the Red Sox and provided a police escort to Fenway Park in time for the game on May 1, 2006?

54. How many times did David Ortiz and Manny Ramirez hit back-to-back home runs during their tenure with the Red Sox?

A. 10

B. 12

C. 14

D. 16

55. What Red Sox hitter holds the mark as baseball's oldest batting champion?

56. Whom did the Red Sox acquire for Jeff Bagwell in the lamentable deal with Houston in July 1990?

57. Who ruptured an Achilles heel on Tony Graffanino's 2005 home run and had to use a pinch-runner before the runs could count on the scoreboard?

A. Alex Cora

B. Gabe Kappler

C. John Olerud

D. Jay Payton

58. Which ballplayer's name appeared on the Fenway Park scoreboard in the film *Field of Dreams*?

A. Vida Blue

B. Archibald "Moonlight" Graham

C. John "Blue Moon" Odom

D. Carl Yastrzemski

59. Please answer the question the candidates for a Massachusetts senate seat all flubbed at a December 2011 political debate: "In what years did the Red Sox win the World Series in this century?"

60. Who holds the Red Sox record for outfield assists in a season?

A. Dom DiMaggio

B. Dwight Evans

C. Harry Hooper

D. Tris Speaker

61. Who holds the Red Sox record for most consecutive games played but was traded in the midst of
that streak?

A. Bobby Doerr

B. Everett Scott

C. Tris Speaker

D. Carl Yastrzemski

62. The 1986 World Series is notorious for a ball going
through a Boston player's legs, but who hit the
grounder in Game 1 that went through a Mets
infielder's legs and brought in the winning run for
the Red Sox?

A. Bill Buckner

B. Rich Gedman

C. Mike Greenwell

D. Jim Rice

63. When was the first year the Red Sox, Bruins and
Celtics all made the postseason in the same year?

64. This Red Sox infielder set a club mark by sacrific-
ing four times in one game, was hired to manage
the next year and, not surprisingly, Boston led the
league in sacrifices. Who was this sacrificial skipper?

A. Jack Barry

B. Bill Carrigan

C. Jimmy Collins

D. Joe Cronin

65. Which Red Sox catcher set a record for most passed balls in 1995?

    A. Bill Hasselman

    B. Scott Hatteberg

    C. Mike Macfarlane

    D. Mike Stanley

66. In decisive Game 5 of the 1999 ALDS Pedro Martinez came out of the bullpen and threw how many hitless innings of relief?

67. What starter got credit for a complete game, did not allow a hit, and still wound up losing for the Red Sox on April 12, 1991?

68. True or false? The Red Sox have never had a losing record against a first-year expansion team.

69. Through 2011, who is the only Red Sox shortstop to hit 40 homers in a season?

70. Who threw nine innings of a Red Sox no-hitter while pitching to only 26 batters?

71. Who holds the Red Sox record for most RBI s in a season?

A. Jimmie Foxx

B. Manny Ramirez

C. Vern Stephens

D. Ted Williams

72. Which of the following obscure Red Sox did *not* represent the club as an All-Star?

A. Tom Brunansky

B. Erik Hanson

C. Jerry Moses

D. Felix Mantilla

73. What U.S. President made a campaign speech at Fenway Park and uttered the line that later proved false: "I have said this before, but I shall say it again and again and again. Your boys are not going to be sent to any foreign wars"?

74. The Red Sox played the first World Series game ever witnessed by a sitting U.S. president. Which president was it?

A. Teddy Roosevelt

B. William Howard Taft

C. Harry Truman

D. Woodrow Wilson

75. The 1999 All-Star Game at Fenway Park, high-lighted by Ted Williams surrounded by adoring players, was one of the more emotional All-Star Game ceremonies. Which league won the game?

76. Which band was the first to hold a full-fledged rock concert at Fenway Park more than 90 years after the place opened?

77. Who tossed a no-hitter in just his second major league start in 2007?

78. True or false? The Red Sox had 18 no-hitters in their first 120 years as a franchise, but none of these were a perfect game.

79. Who singled in the Division Series-clinching run in walkoff fashion in 2008?
   A. Jason Bay
   B. Jed Lowrie
   C. David Ortiz
   D. Kevin Youklis

80. Who came within two outs of a no-hitter for the Red Sox after drilling a batter in the first inning to start a brawl?

81. The Red Sox staged the greatest single-game postseason comeback in 79 years by rallying from 7-0 down in the seventh to beat which team?

A. Cleveland Indians

B. New York Yankees

C. Oakland A's

D. Tampa Bay Rays

82. When was the first year the Red Sox finished in first place but did not play in the World Series?

83. What are the most losses the Red Sox have endured in a season?

A. 100

B. 103

C. 107

D. 111

84. Ted Williams holds the record for most times leading the American League in walks. Four Red Sox hitters since Teddy Ballgame have led the league in bases on balls. Name three of them.

85. The first Yankees-Red Sox trade in 14 years brought New York's designated hitter to Boston in 1986. Who was this former MVP?

86. Who hit a home run in the ninth inning of Game 5 of the 1986 ALCS to put the Red Sox ahead and then hit a game-winning sacrifice fly in the 11th to bring Boston back from seeming elimination?

87. Next to Ted Williams, which Red Sox hitter has produced the highest batting average in a season?
A. Dale Alexander
B. Wade Boggs
C. Nomar Garciaparra
D. Tris Speaker

88. How many consecutive games did the Red Sox win at Fenway Park after Joe Morgan took over as manager of the Red Sox in July 1988?
A. 18
B. 21
C. 24
D. 27

89. Name the one righty and one lefty who earned their 300th career wins with the Olde Town Team.

90. Through 2011, which Massachusetts native is the only pitcher to earn his 300th career save with the Red Sox?

91. Name the only three pitchers who have suffered more than 100 losses while wearing a Red Sox uniform.

92. Which Red Sox pitcher set a record for most consecutive innings without being relieved?
   A. Bill Dinneen
   B. Carl Mays
   C. Smoky Joe Wood
   D. Cy Young

93. Who was the first Red Sox slugger to crack 30 home runs?
   A. Jimmie Foxx
   B. Buck Freeman
   C. Babe Ruth
   D. Ted Williams

94. Which Red Sox third baseman did not commit an error in more than 1,000 chances during a season as a first baseman?
   A. Rico Petrocelli
   B. George Scott
   C. John Valentin
   D. Kevin Youklis

95. True or false? Roger Clemens struck out the last batter in both of his 20-strikeout games.

96. The Red Sox had the earliest start time of a major league game on American soil in American League history. At what hour was the first pitch?

97. What team did the Red Sox open the 2008 season with in Tokyo with a 6:10 A.M. first pitch East Coast Time?

    A. New York Yankees

    B. Oakland A's

    C. Seattle Mariners

    D. Tampa Bay Rays

98. What is the franchise record for most innings thrown by a pitcher in one game?

    A. 15

    B. 18

    C. 21

    D. 24

99. True or false? David Ortiz has served as DH longer than any Red Sox player in history.

100. Which Red Sox player has won the most Gold Glove Awards?

    A. Dwight Evans

    B. Fred Lynn

    C. Frank Malzone

    D. Carl Yastrzemski

Answers on pages 240-250

Red Sox by the Numbers

1. Who is number 1 retired for in Boston?

2. Who donned number 2 longer than anyone else in Boston?
   A. Jacoby Ellsbury
   B. Doug Griffin
   C. Brad Mills
   D. Jerry Remy

3. What uniform number did Hall of Fame manager Joe McCarthy wear while piloting the Red Sox between 1948 and 1950?

4. Unscramble the retired numbers to match the numerical pattern of retired uniform numbers in right field at Fenway that for many years coincided with the opening of the last victorious Red Sox World Series.
   A. 1
   B. 4
   C. 8
   D. 9

5. Which prime number did Keith Foulke have on his back when he threw the final pitch—and fielded the last out—of the curse-curing 2004 World Series?
   A. 17
   B. 29
   C. 37
   D. 43

6. Tom Seaver, the only player with a number retired by the Mets, wore that familiar number in his final stint in the majors with the 1986 Red Sox. What number was it?

   A. 14

   B. 37

   C. 41

   D. 42

7. Which number did Jacoby Ellsbury wear for his first three years in the majors before switching to number 2 in 2010?

   A. 4

   B. 14

   C. 44

   D. 46

8. What uniform number did Tim Wakefield wear to honor the patron saint of knuckleball pitchers?

9. True or false? No Red Sox player ever wore number 9 after Ted Williams joined the team.

Answers on pages 250-251

Your Father's Sox

1. The Red Sox purchased two All-Stars from the Oakland A's at the 1976 trading deadline, but Commissioner Bowie Kuhn disallowed the sale. Who were these two A's?

2. In 1977 Fenway Park's seating capacity became the smallest in the majors after the closing of which stadium?

   A. Connie Mack Stadium

   B. Exhibition Stadium

   C. Forbes Field

   D. Jarry Park

3. Which manager was hired to replace Dick Williams two seasons after the "Impossible Dream" pennant in 1967?

   A. Darrell Johnson

   B. Eddie Kasko

   C. Pete Runnels

   D. Don Zimmer

4. Who penned this line about the sad Sox end to 1977: "The game begins in the spring, when everything else begins again, and it blossoms in the summer, filling the afternoons and evenings, and then as soon as the chill rains come, it stops and leaves you to face the fall alone."

5. True or false? Despite losing the one-game playoff to the Yankees, the 1978 Red Sox actually won the season series from the Yankees.

6. In fateful 1978, the AL East was extremely tight, with four teams winning at least 90 games. Name these four '78 AL East teams (two of those are gimmees).

7. Who kicked off Boston's pennant-winning 1986 season with a leadoff home run in the first game?
   A. Marty Barrett
   B. Wade Boggs
   C. Dwight Evans
   D. Glenn Hoffman

8. Which 1970s Red Sox All-Star was known as "The Rooster"?

9. Who made the heartbreaking final out in both the 1975 World Series and the 1978 one-game playoff for the Red Sox?

10. Which manager was hired to replace Don Zimmer?
    A. Ralph Houk
    B. Darrell Johnson
    C. John McNamara
    D. Joe Morgan

11. Which Red Sox manager was the first to write a designated hitter on a lineup card in 1973?
   A. Darrell Johnson
   B. Eddie Kasko
   C. Dick Williams
   D. Don Zimmer

12. What future Hall of Famer was the first designated hitter in Red Sox history?
   A. Orlando Cepeda
   B. Cecil Cooper
   C. Ben Oglivie
   D. Carl Yastrzemski

13. True or false? When a record 12 American league pitchers won 20 games in 1973, none of these hurlers was on the Red Sox.

14. True or false? The 1978 Red Sox had baseball's best home record.

15. How many years did Mike Torrez pitch for the Red Sox after his ill-fated moment in the 1978 one-game playoff?
   A. 0
   B. 2 years
   C. 4 years
   D. 6 years

16. When Carl Yastrzemski played his 3,000th game with the Red Sox on May 25, 1981, he faced a pitcher who had tossed a perfect game two starts earlier. Who was it?

    A. Len Barker

    B. Tom Browning

    C. Kenny Rogers

    D. Mike Witt

17. What pitcher injured his shoulder during the legendary brawl between the Red Sox and Yankees in May of 1976?

18. True or false? Through 2011, Luis Tiant is the only player in history to earn the Babe Ruth Award for a losing team in the World Series.

19. Who was the last Red Sox pitcher to homer before the designated hitter became the law of the land?

    A. Ken Brett

    B. Bill Lee

    C. Marty Pattin

    D. Luis Tiant

20. True or false? Carl Yastrzemski was the first American League player to collect 400 home runs and 3,000 hits.

Answers on pages 251-254

Out of Left Field

1. Who was the last regular Red Sox left fielder before Ted Williams?

   A. Doc Cramer

   B. Dom DiMaggio

   C. Jimmie Foxx

   D. Joe Vosmik

2. Which left fielder was Duffy's Cliff named after in the early years of Fenway Park?

   A. Frank Duffy

   B. Hugh Duffy

   C. Duffy Dyer

   D. Duffy Lewis

3. Which Boston left fielder finished as runner-up in the American League MVP balloting in 1988 but never appeared in the top 10 in any other year's voting?

   A. Mike Greenwell

   B. Manny Ramirez

   C. Troy O'Leary

   D. Bobby Veach

4. Which legendary left fielder actually pitched in a game for Boston?

   A. Mike Greenwell

   B. Manny Ramirez

   C. Ted Williams

   D. Carl Yastrzemski

5. What Red Sox left fielder is tied with Baltimore's Brooks Robinson for most seasons with one team?

6. Two Red Sox left fielders have hit 40 home runs in a season three times. Name them.

7. Who has played the most career games in left field for the Red Sox?
   A. Mike Greenwell
   B. Jim Rice
   C. Ted Williams
   D. Carl Yastrzemski

8. How many U.S. presidents served in office during Carl Yastrzemski's illustrious Red Sox career?

9. What author penned the tribute *Hub Fans Bid Kid Adieu* to Red Sox left fielder Ted Williams about his final game in 1960?

Answers on pages 254-255

Your Grandfather's Sox

1. What year did Ted Williams debut with the Red Sox?
   A. 1938
   B. 1939
   C. 1940
   D. 1941

2. What Hall of Famer and former Red Sox pitcher fanned Ted Williams twice in the Kid's 1939 debut?

3. Who is the only pitcher to ever win 20 games for a last-place Red Sox club?
   A. Howard Ehmke
   B. Wes Ferrell
   C. Boo Ferriss
   D. Bill Monbouquette

4. Who was the future Hall of Fame shortstop traded by the Red Sox in 1939?

5. The Red Sox hammered not one but two Hall of Fame pitchers while rallying from a 10-0 deficit on August 28, 1950 against which team?
   A. Cleveland Indians
   B. New York Yankees
   C. St. Louis Browns
   D. Washington Senators

6. Which pitcher was thrown into a holding cell at Fenway Park on the day he signed his first contract with the Red Sox?

   A. Bill Lee

   B. Bill Monbouquette

   C. Babe Ruth

   D. Jonathon Papelbon

7. True or false? Ted Williams is the only hitter in major league history to win the Triple Crown twice.

8. When Ted Williams returned from the Korean War late in the 1953 at age 35 after having survived a crash landing, what did he hit in the 37 games he played?

   A. .197

   B. .254

   C. .344

   D. .407

9. Which year did 18-time All-Star Ted Williams hit the walkoff All-Star homer that provided what he considered the greatest thrill of his career?

   A. 1941

   B. 1946

   C. 1951

   D. 1956

10. Who was the only Red Sox pitcher to win 20 games both before and after serving in World War II?

A. Joe Dobson

B. Boo Ferriss

C. Tex Hughson

D. Mel Parnell

11. With the Red Sox needing to win one of the last two games of 1949 at Yankee Stadium to win the pennant, the Red Sox lost both. Who were the two 20-game winners that could not lift the Sox in the Bronx?

12. The Red Sox were lamentably the last team to integrate. Who was their first African American player?

13. Which year did the Red Sox score 1,000 runs for the first time?

A. 1938

B. 1941

C. 1946

D. 1950

14. True or false? Ted Williams was never ejected from a game as a player.

15. Who devised the "Williams Shift" while managing another club and later managed Teddy Ballgame in Boston?

16. Who surrendered the fabled final Ted Williams home run in the Kid's last major league at bat on September 28, 1960?
    A. Steve Barber
    B. Jack Fisher
    C. Mike Fornieles
    D. Tracy Stallard

17. During his legendary 1941 season, did Ted Williams bat .400 on the road?

18. Which outfielder made the throw to Johnny Pesky that became infamous in Boston on the game-winning hit in the bottom of the eighth inning in Game 7 of the 1946 World Series?
    A. Lee Culberson
    B. Dom DiMaggio
    C. Bob Klinger
    D. Ted Williams

19. Whose club record for RBIs did Jimmie Foxx break when he drove in 175 in 1938?

20. Whose record for most strikeouts in a game did Roger Clemens shatter in 1986 with 20 strikeouts?

A. Mickey McDermott

B. Bill Monbouquette

C. Smoky Joe Wood

D. Cy Young

Answers on pages 255-257

Octobers — Great and Tragic

1. Which Oakland pitcher started—and lost—twice in Boston's 1975 ALCS three-game sweep of the three-time defending world champions?

   A. Vida Blue

   B. Ken Holtzman

   C. Catfish Hunter

   D. Blue Moon Odom

2. Who was the winning pitcher in fabled Game 6 of the 1975 World Series?

   A. Jim Burton

   B. Reggie Cleveland

   C. Jim Willoughby

   D. Rick Wise

3. Who took the loss in crushing Game 7 of the 1975 World Series for the Red Sox?

   A. Jim Burton

   B. Reggie Cleveland

   C. Jim Willoughby

   D. Rick Wise

4. What was the last year the Red Sox clinched a world championship at home?

5. Who hit the first Fenway Park postseason home run in 34 years for the Red Sox during the 1946 World Series?

   A. Dom DiMaggio

   B. Bobby Doerr

   C. Ted Williams

   D. Rudy York

6. Who is the only pitcher to toss a one-hitter for the Red Sox in the World Series?

7. What Red Sox hurler holds the mark for most innings pitched in a World Series game and also tossed 29 2/3 consecutive World Series shutout innings?

8. Which Red Sox player has appeared in the most World Series games in franchise history?

   A. Dwight Evans

   B. Harry Hooper

   C. Duffy Lewis

   D. Jason Varitek

9. Through 2011 the Red Sox have won seven World Series, all against different National League teams. Name all seven clubs the Sox have vanquished for the title.

Answers on pages 257-258

Your Great-Grandfather's Sox

1. Which local college played the Red Sox in the first game ever played at Fenway Park in 1912?
    A. Boston College
    B. Boston University
    C. Harvard
    D. Northeastern

2. The 1915 Red Sox had such a talented pitching staff that 18-8 southpaw Babe Ruth didn't pitch in the World Series. What team did the Sox beat in the Series?

3. How many times did Babe Ruth take the mound as Boston's opening day starting pitcher?

4. Whose inside-the-park home run in the bottom of the 10th inning tied Game 2 before it was called by darkness, eventually forcing an eighth and deciding game in the 1912 World Series?
    A. Larry Gardner
    B. Harry Hooper
    C. Duffy Lewis
    D. Tris Speaker

5. What Hall of Famer was the first Red Sox manager in 1901?
    A. Jimmy Collins
    B. Chick Stahl
    C. Jake Stahl
    D. Cy Young

6. How many times did Cy Young win 20 games in his eight years with the Red Sox?

7. Boston set a franchise record in 1906 by losing how many games in a row?
   A. 11
   B. 14
   C. 17
   D. 20

8. Who was the first Red Sox slugger to lead the league in home runs?
   A. Buck Freeman
   B. Babe Ruth
   C. Tris Speaker
   D. Jake Stahl

9. Babe Ruth led or tied for most home runs with the Red Sox in four of his five full seasons with the Red Sox. How many homers did he hit that one season where he missed the home run lead?
   A. 2
   B. 5
   C. 8
   D. 11

10. Back in the Deadball Era, Boston's arms were very much alive. Which pitcher set the mark for lowest ERA in a season in club history in 1914?

A. Dutch Leonard

B. Babe Ruth

C. Smoky Joe Wood

D. Cy Young

11. Who has the lowest career ERA in Red Sox history?

A. Dutch Leonard

B. Babe Ruth

C. Smoky Joe Wood

D. Cy Young

12. After being knocked out in Game 7, this pitcher came out of the bullpen to win deciding Game 8 in 1912. Who was he?

A. Hugh Bedient

B. Rube Foster

C. Smoky Joe Wood

D. Cy Young

13. Whose "walkoff" sacrifice fly ended the 1912 World Series for the Red Sox?

A. Larry Gardner

B. Harry Hooper

C. Duffy Lewis

D. Tris Speaker

14. Where did the Red Sox play before Fenway Park became home?

15. Who became the first full-time coach in Red Sox history in 1916?
    A. Jimmy Burke
    B. High Duffy
    C. Lefty Leifield
    D. Heinie Wagner

16. The two Red Sox pitchers who faced the most batters in a season were both on the same staff in 1902. Bill Dinneen was one. Who was the other?

17. In Babe Ruth's last season with the Red Sox—and his first season as an everyday player—he broke the major league mark for home runs with how many?
    A. 11
    B. 19
    C. 29
    D. 54

18. The 1918 world champion Red Sox hold the club record for most times being shut out. How many times did the world champs get blanked?
    A. 14
    B. 18
    C. 22
    D. 26

19. A former Red Sox pitcher was banned for life for his part in the Black Sox Scandal in Chicago during the 1919 World Series. Who was he?

20. The year after Babe Ruth left, Harry Hooper led the Red Sox in home runs with how many?

A. 4

B. 7

C. 11

D. 14

Answers on pages 258-260

Red Sox Answers

Red Sox Basics

1. Jim Rice. He hit 46 homers and banged out 15 triples in his MVP season of 1978 for the Sox. The last player before Rice to reach those numbers was Yankee Joe DiMaggio in 1937.

2. A. Jimmie Foxx. Old Double-X reached 40 homers three times with the Philadelphia Athletics and hit 41 for the 1936 Red Sox. He crushed 50 home runs two years later.

3. Babe Ruth. He mostly pitched for the Red Sox between 1914-1919, but you'll never find a better-hitting pitcher.

4. B. 1999. The Yankees won the ALCS in five games. (The 1978 one-game playoff counts as a regular-season game.)

5. A. Bob Bailey. His 17-year career ended with a strikeout against Goose Gossage as a pinch hitter in the seventh inning on October 3, 1978.

6. False. Dom DiMaggio achieved the feat in 1950. In an era without much base stealing, he led the AL with just 15 steals (he tied for the lead with 11 triples). In 2009 Ellsbury led the AL with 70 steals and tied for the top spot with 10 triples.

7. B. Jim Rice. In his lone 40-homer year, Rice won the MVP but fanned 126 times. Teddy Ballgame managed the feat in 1949, Rico followed suit in 1969, and Yaz did it twice (1967 and 1970).

8. Jimmie Foxx. Double-X hit 50 in 1938.

9. Wade Boggs (.338) and Tris Speaker (.337).

10. Jimmie Foxx, Ted Williams and Manny Ramirez. Foxx, who hit 222 homers for Boston, clubbed his 500th on September 24, 1940 against his old team, the Philadelphia A's. Ted Williams hit the 500th of his 521 Red Sox homers on June 17, 1960, against Cleveland. Ramirez, with 274 of his homers with

Boston, connected for number 500 on May 31, 2008 against Baltimore.

11. C. Show them he was wearing a uniform. All the options are ludicrous, but this one is true. Terry Francona was indeed wearing his jersey under his ever-present wind jacket and was understandably angry about the trivial midgame interruption. He was later ejected from that game… for arguing about a call on the bases.

12. Bob Stanley. The Stanley Steamer saved 132 for the Red Sox in the 1970s and 1980s.

13. B. Reggie Jackson. He hit 51 home runs against the Red Sox, including 25 at Fenway Park, among his 563 career home runs.

14. Four. Jason Varitek also caught no-hitters for Hideo Nomo (2001), Derek Lowe (2002) and Clay Buchholz (2007). Curt Schilling and Pedro Martinez lost no-hitters in the ninth, and Davern Hansack threw five hitless innings before rain halted the effort. White Sox Hall of Famer Ray Schalk had a fourth no-no broken up in extra innings.

15. B. Ed Barrow. Barrow took over for Jack Barry when the latter joined the Army in World War I. Barrow's Bosox won the 1918 World Series. Ironically, it was Barrow who, as Yankees general manager, would arrange for the transfer of many of the best Red Sox players to the Yankees in the 1920s.

16. C. Bill Carrigan. He won the 1915 and 1916 World Series as manager of the Red Sox.

17. C. John McNamara. He won the 1986 AL Manager of the Year Award, the first Sox manager so honored. Jimy Williams followed him in 1999.

18. Virginia (1901), Georgia (1902-1906, 1932), Arkansas (1907-10, 1912-18, 1920-23), California (1911), Florida (1919, 1928-31, 1933-42, 1946-58, 1966-present), Texas (1924), Louisiana (1925-27), Massachusetts (1943-44), New Jersey (1945) and Arizona (1959-65).

19. C. Grady Little. The much-maligned manager split his 12 postseason games with the Sox in 2003, going 6-6, though he was fired after the last loss in the ALCS. Jimy Williams managed the most postseason games of the quartet, but he went just 5-9 in the Octobers of 1998 and 1999. Kevin Kennedy went 0-3 in 1995, and Butch Hobson never reached the postseason.

20. B. Pedro Martinez. Pedro won a 13-3 laugher in Cleveland in the opener of the 1998 Division Series to end a 13-game postseason streak that began in 1986 and included getting swept in the 1988, 1990 and 1995 postseasons. The Indians got the last laugh, though, winning the next three ALDS games in '98.

21. It is a ground-rule triple, the only such triple in the ground rules at any major league park.

22. B. Gary Gaetti. On July 17, 1990, the Twins third baseman started two around-the-horn triple plays as Minnesota won, 1-0. Gaetti joined the Red Sox for the last stop on a 20-year journey of the majors in 2000.

23. Jimmy Fallon. He played Ben Wrightman, obsessed with the Sox and his girlfriend, played by Drew Barrymore.

24. Because the Red Sox won the World Series! The directors, life-long Red Sox fans Bob and Peter Farrelly, couldn't let the chance for the perfect real-life ending go by.

25. A. 10. The Red Sox reached double digits—and knocked out two pitchers—before the Marlins recorded an out at Fenway Park. Eleven straight men reached to open the game and Johnny Damon became the first player with a single, double and triple in one inning in a 14-run frame that became a 25-8 rout.

26. Tom Gordon. In the number-one bestseller, *The Girl Who Loved Tom Gordon*, a girl lost in the woods thinks of the 1990s Sox reliever she adores as she tries to survive. Gordon hurt his arm and later pitched for the Yankees—wonder if the girl still loved him?

27. Jim Lonborg. Lonborg led the AL with 22 wins and 246 strikeouts in 39 starts, the last coming on the final day of the season to claim the 1967 pennant. An unfortunate skiing accident that winter kept him from reaching that level again for the Sox, though he later excelled with the Phillies.

28. B. Dalton Jones. Jones played pretty regularly from 1964 to 1966, but it was in 1967, when the Sox suddenly contended, that he played less but his hits meant more. He hit .277 off the bench (13-for-47) during the "Impossible Dream" season and thrived in a pinch in Boston through 1969.

29. C. Wally Schang. Schang hit .244 in 1918 but batted 200 points higher in the World Series in his first season after

coming over from the Athletics. He hit .306 in 1919 and reached that mark five more times in his career, though only once more with Boston.

30. D. Harry Hooper. Hall of Fame Hoop piled up the stolen bases—and the world championships—with Boston between 1909 and 1919. He was also a superb outfielder.

31. False. Billy Werber led the AL in 1934-35. His 69 steals over those two years, however, wound up one stolen base shy of Jacoby Ellsbury's 70 in 2009, Jacoby's second straight year leading the league.

32. Two. He won the 1999 and 2000 Cy Youngs with the Red Sox, finished second two other times (1998, 2002), third once (2003) and fourth another year (2004).

33. Tony Armas and Carl Pavano. Armas, the Venezuelan-born son of 1980s Sox slugger Tony Armas, pitched 10 so-so years, mostly with Montreal/Washington. Pavano, from Southington, Connecticut, surpassed 100 career wins (and losses) in an itinerant career marred by injuries.

34. C. Reggie Smith. He was the first Sox player to turn the trick (in 1967), and the only one to do so four times. It was 22 years between Smith's last time and Luis Alicea's only career two-way feat in 1995.

35. B. Bill Mueller. He'd already hit a solo homer on July 29, 2003, when he connected for a grand slam from the right side against Aaron Fultz in Texas in the seventh. An inning later he homered from the left side with the bases full against Jay Powell in a 14-7 win.

36. Ted Williams. Teddy Ballgame won six batting titles (1941-42, 1947-48, 1957-58); Wade Boggs won five (1983, 1985-88).

37. B. Bill LeFebvre. A pitcher, LeFebvre homered in his first—and only—at bat in 1938 during a relief appearance. He never hit another home run, but he did bat .276. His 5.05 ERA kept those at bats under 100 for his brief career.

38. D. 32. Injuries limited Jacoby Ellsbury to just 83 plate appearances in 2010 with no home runs and a .192 average. Nine homers in 2008 had been his highest output prior to his 32 homers in 2011.

39. A. Tom Gordon. He saved 46 games for the 1998 Red Sox, including a club-record 43 in a row that year and 54 straight over two seasons. Shortly after the streak ended in June 1999,

Flash blew out his elbow and never saved another game for the Sox. He did, however, pitch nine more seasons for six more teams.

40. Babe Ruth. The Babe tossed 105 complete games to 100 by Roger Clemens. Of course, Ruth pitched in an era when complete games were far more common, but the Babe made 239 fewer starts than the Rocket for the Olde Towne Team.

41. The first dozen. Boston lost the first six games of 2011 and stood at 2-10 on April 15. Boston played .616 ball (85-53) over the next 138 games, eventually building a 9 ½-game lead in the Wild Card. Unfortunately, a 3-9 finish handed Tampa Bay the postseason spot. And that's all we'll say about that.

42. True. No one who managed the Red Sox ever managed the Mets until Bobby Valentine, who managed New York from 1996 to 2002. Connecticut's own Bobby V. is the only manager to take the Mets to the postseason in consecutive seasons (1999-2000).

43. C. 45. That list includes Cy Young, who reluctantly managed for six games in 1907.

44. D. 11. Most were elected for their playing exploits or overall managing career with several teams, but it is an impressive list: Ed Barrow, Lou Boudreau, Frank Chance, Jimmy Collins, Joe Cronin, Hugh Duffy, Bucky Harris, Billy Herman, Joe McCarthy, Dick Williams and Cy Young.

45. A. Wade Boggs. He had 200 hits and 100 walks for four straight years (1986-89). And if he'd drawn four more walks in 1985, it would been five straight.

46. Nomar Garciaparra, Manny Ramirez and Bill Mueller. Garciaparra won titles in 1999-2000, batting .357 and .372, respectively. After Ichiro Suzuki won in 2001 as a Mariners rookie, Manny Ramirez reclaimed the 2002 crown for Boston at .349. Manny almost won again the following year, but Mueller beat him by a point (.326-.325).

47. Cy Young and Pedro Martinez. Cy went 33-10 with a 1.68 ERA and 158 K's in 1901, the AL's inaugural season. In 1999 Pedro went 23-4 with a 2.07 ERA and 313 strikeouts to win the Cy Young Award. (Note: Roger Clemens twice won the Triple Crown, but it happened with Toronto.)

48. Roger Clemens, Ferguson Jenkins, Pedro Martinez, Curt Schilling and John Smoltz each rang up 3,000 strikeouts

before allowing 1,000 walks. (Jenkins, Pedro and Schilling never reached four-digits in walks.) The only other pitcher to achieve this feat was Greg Maddux.

49. Jacob Ellsbury. He collected 32 homers, 39 steals, 105 RBIs, and a .321 average in 2011.

50. Ted Williams. Teddy Ballgame's blast in the right-field bleachers bounced off the head of a patron, Joseph A. Boucher, in Section 42, Row 37, Seat 21. The ball broke Boucher's straw hat, leaving him bruised and angry. "How far away must one sit to be safe in this park?" fumed Boucher, who did not get the ball.

51. Tim Wakefield. The knuckleballer, who rekindled his career after signing with the 1995 Red Sox, surpassed 3,000 innings with Boston in 2011.

52. C. Red Ruffing. He absorbed a club-record 25 defeats in 1928, followed by 22 more L's in '29 before being sent to the Yankees, where he won 231 games and six World Series rings.

53. Doug Mirabelli. Traded to San Diego in December 2005, the backup catcher was soon brought back because his replacement could not catch Tim Wakefield's knuckleball. In a trade GM Theo Epstein came to regret, San Diego received reliever Cla Meredith and catcher Josh Bard, who could handle a staff, just not a knuckleball.

54. A. 10. Big Papi and Manny's mark for successive home runs in five-plus seasons together in Boston is six homers shy of Yankees Babe Ruth and Lou Gehrig and Braves Hank Aaron and Eddie Mathews.

55. Ted Williams. He clinched the 1958 batting title several weeks after his 39th birthday. The Kid won it again the following year at 40.

56. Larry Andersen. The reliever had a 1.23 ERA in 15 appearances to help the Red Sox win a division title, but he blew a save and lost the first game in Oakland's ALCS sweep and then signed with San Diego. Jeff Bagwell was 1991 NL Rookie of the Year and hit 449 homers as an Astro.

57. B. Gabe Kappler. Signed by the Red Sox after being released by the Yomiuri Giants, he was out of action until June 2006. He retired, managed for the Red Sox in the minors, came back, and played three more years with Milwaukee and Tampa Bay.

58. B. Archibald "Moonlight" Graham. The actual ballplayer played one game with the 1905 New York Giants but never batted. The fictional character, played by Bert Lancaster in the film, was a doctor from Minnesota who was, well, dead.

59. 2004 and 2007. Now if you can answer that question and survive the scathing attack ads, you, too, can spend the next six years in Washington.

60. D. Tris Speaker. The Grey Eagle, who played a notoriously shallow center field, recorded 35 outfield assists in both 1909 and 1912. The Hall of Famer owns the major league mark with 449 outfield assists, 207 with Boston. He also recorded 64 of his 139 double plays with the Sox.

61. B. Everett Scott. He played 932 consecutive games from June 20, 1916 to October 2, 1921. He was traded to the Yankees and played another 375 straight games until 1925. His overall streak of 1,307 stood as the major league record, until it was shattered by Yankees teammate "Iron Man" Lou Gehrig.

62. B. Rich Gedman. His grounder went through the legs of Mets second baseman Tim Teufel at frigid Shea Stadium to score the game's lone run. Bruce Hurst and Calvin Schiraldi combined on a 1-0 shutout.

63. 1975. It was the year the Red Sox won the pennant, the Bruins reached the playoffs in the Adams Division, and the Celtics won the NBA Atlantic Division. None of the teams won the title. In case you're wondering, the '75 Patriots finished last.

64. A. Jack Barry. Barry, who bunted runners over four times on August 21, 1916, took over as manager the following year after Bill Carrigan's retirement. In Barry's lone season as skipper, the 1917 Sox sacrificed 310 times, by far the most in the league. Barry's 54 sacs led the team but was still 13 off the league lead. He left to fight in World War I and later coached Holy Cross to an .800 winning percentage over 40 seasons.

65. C. Mike MacFarlane. His record 25 passed balls just so happened to coincide with the Boston debut of the city's greatest knuckleballer: Tim Wakefield.

66. Six. Pedro Martinez came out of the pen in the fourth inning and did not allow a hit the rest of the way. He entered the 8-8 game after Bret Saberhagen and Derek Lowe were tattooed, but Pedro remained until the job was done and the Red Sox won, 12-8.

67. Matt Young. He walked seven in a 2-1 loss in Cleveland. And, even more bad luck, 1991 was the year Major League Baseball declared a pitcher (or a team) had to play nine innings to get credit for a no-hitter.

68. True. Though it took a three-run rally in the last inning of the last game against the 1969 Seattle Pilots (later the Milwaukee Brewers) to go 6-6. Otherwise Boston won the season series with the expansion Angels (11-7) and Senators (10-8) in 1961; the Royals (10-1) in 1969; the Mariners (10-1) and Blue Jays (12-3) in 1977; and Tampa Bay (9-3) in 1998.

69. Rico Petrocelli. He clubbed 40 homers for the 1969 season as the team's shortstop. That tied Carl Yastrzemski for the team lead.

70. Ernie Shore. He came on in relief in the top of the first inning after Babe Ruth was ejected for arguing balls and strikes on June 23, 1917. The runner was thrown out stealing, and Shore retired all 26 batters for the joint no-hitter.

71. A. Jimmie Foxx. Double X knocked home 175, along with 50 homers and a .346 average in 1938. Only Hank Greenberg's 58 homers for Detroit kept Foxx from claiming his second Triple Crown. Vern Stephens and Ted Williams are the only Red Sox hitters to come close to the mark, both knocking in 159 in 1949.

72. A. Tom Brunansky. Bruno—who came in return for saves machine Lee Smith in 1990—never made the All-Star team for Boston, though he made it once as a Twin. Erik Hanson (1995) and Jerry Moses (1970) were actually Sox All-Stars but did not play in the game. Felix Mantilla went 0-for-2 in the 1965 game.

73. Franklin D. Roosevelt. He made the speech at Fenway days before his re-election to a record third term in 1940. On December 7, 1941, Pearl Harbor rendered all past promises moot.

74. D. Woodrow Wilson. The President saw the Red Sox beat the Phillies at the Baker Bowl in Game 2 of the 1915 World Series. The Red Sox won, 2-1. William Howard Taft attended regular-season contests only.

75. American League. Back when the All-Star Game was simply an exhibition with no World Series repercussions, the AL was a 4-1 winner in 1999. Pedro Martinez fanned the first four batters to earn MVP, but he soon wound up on the disabled list.

76. Bruce Springsteen and the E-Street Band. Bruce's name was carved into the field when he played for two nights in September 2003.

77. Clay Buchholz. He was just the third pitcher in history to toss a no-no so early in his career. His September 1, 2007, gem against Baltimore was preserved by a wicked stop by Dustin Pedroia at Fenway. Buchholz tossed the 17th no-hitter in Red Sox annals.

78. False. The team's first no-hitter by Cy Young over the Philadelphia Athletics on May 5, 1904, was the first perfecto in American League history.

79. B. Jed Lowrie. The shortstop singled home Jason Bay, who barely beat the throw, in the bottom of the ninth of Game 4 to give Boston its third postseason series victory against the Angels since 2004 (and fourth since 1986).

80. Pedro Martinez. Pedro hit Tampa Bay leadoff man Gerald Williams, who stared at his hand before rushing the mound. Williams was ejected but Martinez retired the next 25 batters, 13 by strikeout, before ex-Boston catcher John Flaherty singled with one out in the ninth. Pedro threw a one-hitter and won in Tampa, 8-0.

81. D. Tampa Bay Rays. Boston trailed 7-0 in the seventh inning of Game 5 of the 2008 ALCS, but the Red Sox came back with four runs in the seventh and three in the eighth before J.D. Drew, who homered earlier, singled in the winner in the ninth to culminate the biggest comeback since Game 4 of the 1929 World Series.

82. 1904. Boston won a tight pennant race over New York, then known as the Highlanders. But another New York team, the Giants, refused to play the World Series against what they deemed an inferior league, which just so happened to have won the first World Series in 1903.

83. D. 111. The 1932 Red Sox went 43-111, recording a franchise-worst .279 "win" percentage. The Sox have endured six triple-digit loss seasons, the last (to date) in 1965.

84. Carl Yastrzemski, Dwight Evans, Wade Boggs and David Ortiz. Yaz led the AL in walks in 1963 and 1968; Evans in 1981, 1985 and 1987; Boggs in 1986 and 1988; and Ortiz in 2006. Prior to Ted Williams, Jimmie Foxx led the AL for Boston in 1938.

85. Don Baylor. The 1979 AL MVP, acquired for Mike Easler, hit .238, but the 20th-century leader in hit-by-pitches set a career-best by getting drilled 35 times in '86. Baylor hit .346 in the ALCS and his ninth-inning home run was crucial in Boston's epic Game 5 comeback.

86. Dave Henderson. Boston was one pitch from losing the pennant when Henderson, a mid-season acquisition from Seattle, homered off Donnie Moore and put the Red Sox ahead. After the Angels tied it, Henderson's sac fly off Moore in the 11th proved to be the winner. Boston won the last three games of the ALCS to win the pennant.

87. D. Tris Speaker. The Hall of Fame outfielder batted .383 for the 1912 world champs. Nomar Garciaparra (2000) and Dale Alexander (1932) each batted .372.

88. C. 24. Morgan Magic was the rule after Joe Morgan took over from John McNamara during the 1988 All-Star break. The Red Sox won an AL-record 24 straight home games, including an 11-0 homestand to start Walpole Joe's managerial career. Boston soon lifted the interim skipper tag.

89. Cy Young and Lefty Grove. Cy was in mid-career when he gained the 300th of his 511 career victories in 1901. And shame on you if you whiffed on Lefty Grove after the big ol' hint provided. He got his 300th and final win for the 1941 Red Sox.

90. Jeff Reardon. The Dalton native, undrafted out of UMass-Amherst, pitched for the Mets, Expos and Twins before earning his 300th save in Boston in 1991. He set the short-lived major league saves record (342) in 1992 with the Red Sox but was traded not long after to the Braves.

91. Roger Clemens (111), Cy Young (112) and Tim Wakefield (168).

92. A. Bill Dinneen. The hero of the first World Series in 1903, he turned into Iron Man in 1904, starting—and finishing—37 games in 335 2/3 innings without relief. Add in full days' work at the end of 1903 and the start of 1905 and it comes to 440 2/3. And that doesn't even count his four complete games in the '03 World Series.

93. A. Jimmie Foxx. Double X was also the first Sox slugger to crack 40 (1936) and 50 (1938). Babe Ruth just missed with 29 in 1919.

94. D. Kevin Youklis. Youk did not make an error at first base in 2007, handling 1,080 chances flawlessly and winning a Gold Glove. At third base, his natural position, he did commit three errors in 13 games in '07. He later moved back to the hot corner.

95. False. Ken Phelps of the Mariners grounded out to end the 1986 game—the only time Phelps put a ball in play at Fenway when Clemens set the single-game K mark. A decade later Clemens fanned final batter Travis Fryman for number 20 in Detroit.

96. 10 A.M. April 20, 1903, Boston opened the season at 10 A.M. The Patriots Day lid lifter was the first part of a separate admission doubleheader. It got the club an early start en route to its first world championship.

97. Oakland A's. Ironically it's the same franchise the Red Sox had the earliest start time against on U.S. soil, in 1903. Though the A's were then calling Philadelphia home. (Note: Other teams have also opened major season in Japan since 2000.)

98. D. 24. On September 1, 1906, Joe Harris went the distance— and lost. The Philadelphia A's scored three times in the top of the 24th after Harris had not allowed a run for 20 straight innings. Harris had plenty of bad luck, going 2-21 for a 49-105 team.

99. True. David Ortiz was designated hitter for the Red Sox for nine straight seasons, through 2011, surpassing 300 homers and 1,000 RBIs while serving as a DH in 1,169 games (plus 118 at first base).

100. A. Dwight Evans. Dewey won the Gold Glove eight times, one more than Carl Yastrzemski. Frank Malzone was the first Red Sox player to win the award, in 1957.

Red Sox by the Numbers

1. Bobby Doerr. The Hall of Fame second baseman hit 223 homers and batted .288 for the Sox in a career that stretched from 1937 to 1951. He actually wore number 9 before Ted Williams, and 20 men followed Doerr in number 1 before it was officially retired in 1988.

2. D. Jerry Remy. Somerset's own Rem-Dawg wore number 2 for six seasons and 710 games as Boston's second baseman. Infielder Doug Griffin wore number 2 for six years and 610

games before Remy's arrival. Coach Brad Mills wore it for five seasons.

3. None. Joe McCarthy never wore a uniform with a number on it during his time with the Cubs (prior to uniform numbers), the Yankees (one of the first teams to don numbers) or the Red Sox (who first wore numbers in 1931).

4. D-B-A-C, or 9-4-1-8, displayed in the order in which the team retired the numbers. It was also interpreted as 9/4/18, the start date of the 1918 World Series, Boston's last championship for 86 years (though the first game of that World Series was actually 9/5/18). The retired uniform numbers were later arranged numerically, and any talk of a curse was quashed in 2004.

5. B. 29. Keith Foulke had also gotten the last out to climax the unprecedented comeback from three games down in the ALCS. He then finished each of the four World Series games to sweep away 86 years without a world championship.

6. C. 41. Tom Seaver wore that number during his 19-year career with the Mets, Reds, White Sox and Red Sox. An injury kept Seaver as a spectator in the Boston dugout during the 1986 World Series against the Mets.

7. D. 46. Rookie Jacoby Ellsbury was wearing number 46 when he helped the Red Sox claim the 2007 World Series. He kept number 46 until longtime number 2, Coach Brad Mills, took the Houston managing job after the 2009 season.

8. 49. Tim Wakefield, and many knuckleball pitchers, have worn number 49 in tribute to Hoyt Wilhelm, the first practitioner of the pitch to reach the Hall of Fame.

9. False. Rookie Ted Williams donned 9 in 1939, but Johnny Peacock and Lou Finney wore it in 1944 while Williams served in World War II. His number was safe during his stint in the Korean War, but pitcher Frank Sullivan was so overheated in a 1955 game in Kansas City that he sweated through several different numbers, including number 9.

Your Father's Sox

1. Rollie Fingers and Joe Rudi. Bowie Kuhn sent both players back to Oakland in "the best interests of baseball," part of an ongoing feud between Kuhn and maverick A's owner Charlie Finley. Both players left the A's after the season as free agents, neither going to Boston.

2. D. Jarry Park. In 1977 the Montreal Expos left their 28,000-seat ballpark for Olympic Stadium, which had room for more than 50,000. That same year the expansion Toronto Blue Jays welcomed major league baseball at Exhibition Stadium, with seating for more than 40,000.

3. B. Eddie Kasko. Coach Eddie Popowski filled out the last few games of the 1969 season, and Eddie Kasko was hired that fall. Though the Sox had winning records four straight years, the Sox would not claim another pennant until 1975, with Darrell Johnson at the helm.

4. A. Bartlett Giamatti. Boston born and raised in South Hadley, Giamatti was a professor of comparative literature at Yale when he penned those lines in 1977. He was named president of the school the following year and president of the National League in 1986. He was baseball commissioner for just five months when he died suddenly at 51.

5. False. The 1978 Red Sox finished 7-9 against New York and would have tied the season series if they'd won the one-game playoff, but let's not go there…

6. New York Yankees (100-63), Boston Red Sox (99-64), Milwaukee Brewers (93-69) and Baltimore Orioles (90-71).

7. C. Dwight Evans. Dewey led off the '86 season with a homer off Jack Morris in Detroit. The Sox cuffed around Morris, but he got the 6-5 win at Tiger Stadium.

8. Rick Burleson. The Red Sox leadoff man and sparkplug shortstop was nicknamed "Rooster" for his reddish hair and fiery demeanor. By contrast, mid-1970s Yankees shortstop Fred Stanley was nicknamed "Chicken."

9. Carl Yastrzemski. Yaz popped up to center field off Will McEnaney to end Game 7 of the 1975 World Series against the Reds at Fenway Park. He popped up to third base off Rich Gossage to end the 1978 one-game playoff against the Yankees. Both games were at Fenway Park.

10. A. Ralph Houk. "The Major" managed the Red Sox from 1981 to 1984 before retiring for good at age 65 and was replaced by John McNamara. A Silver Star recipient at the Battle of the Bulge, Houk really was a major. He went 312-282 with the Red Sox and had a .514 winning percentage in 20 years managing the Yankees, Tigers and Sox.

11. B. Eddie Kasko. He was also the first manager to hand in a lineup card with a DH listed in a major league game. Though you could call it a tie with Yankees manager—and future Red Sox skipper—Ralph Houk on April 6, 1973. Houk's DH, Ron Blomberg, made history at Fenway Park with a walk in the top of the first.

12. A. Orlando Cepeda. Though all four were members of the '73 Sox, Cepeda was the primary DH from day one. Released by world champion Oakland days before the DH became the new law of the American League, Cepeda's knees made it impossible to play the field. The former MVP agreed to be Boston's first DH, hitting .289 with 20 home runs and 86 RBIs in 143 games—much better numbers than any pitcher.

13. False. Luis Tiant won 20 games for the Red Sox in 1973, one of a dozen 20-game winners during the first year that the designated hitter was enacted.

14. True. The Red Sox went 59-23 at home, and that included the one-game playoff loss to the Yankees. Boston's 40-41 road record is what did them in.

15. C. 4 years. Mike Torrez had a 60-54 record in 161 games with the Red Sox, pitching longer for Boston than for any team in his 18-season career. The Red Sox traded him to the Mets before the 1983 season.

16. A. Len Barker. The Cleveland righty had thrown the first perfect game in 13 years against Toronto on May 15, 1981. Despite having a 4-0 lead at Fenway, it was the only time in a 10-game span that Barker did not pitch into the ninth. Carl Yastrzemski contributed an RBI single and slid in with the winning run in the ninth in game 3,000.

17. Bill Lee. During the brawl, Yankees third baseman Graig Nettles grinded the lefty's shoulder repeatedly into the ground, body slammed him, and then punched Lee in the face. The Red Sox rallied to win the first game between the clubs at refurbished Yankee Stadium, but Lee was lost for two months and was never again the same pitcher.

18. True. The Babe Ruth Award, first given in 1949, has gone to a player on the winning World Series team every year except one. El Tiante pitched three times in the 1975 Series—all Boston wins—going the distance twice and starting epic Game 6 against the Reds. (A separate MVP Award has been given since 1955—in '75 it went to Pete Rose.)

19. C. Marty Pattin. Though Ken Brett, George's brother and a sensational-hitting pitcher, was the last Red Sox pitcher with a multi-homer game in 1971, Pattin went deep on September 26, 1972, in the final days before the DH rule.

20. True. Yaz hit his 400th home run on July 24, 1979, off Oakland's Mike Morgan. He collected his 3,000th hit a few weeks later against Yankee Jim Beattie, a Sox fan as a kid in Maine. Yaz was the first AL player to reach the 400-3,000 plateau, joining Stan Musial, Willie Mays and Hank Aaron in the NL. Others would follow.

Out of Left Field

1. D. Joe Vosmik. Vosmik actually played left field when Ted Williams was a rookie—with Ted playing right in 1939. The Red Sox sold Vosmik to Brooklyn in 1940, moved Williams to left—less ground to cover—and let veteran Doc Cramer and rookie Dom DiMaggio take turns manning the other two spots.

2. D. Duffy Lewis. When it opened in 1912 Fenway Park had an incline in left field that was mastered by incumbent left fielder Duffy Lewis, a three-time Red Sox world champion.

3. A. Mike Greenwell. Greenie placed a distant second to Oakland's Jose Canseco in the 1988 MVP race and never finished in the top 10 in the voting again. Manny Ramirez finished in the top 10 in the MVP seven times with the Sox, though he never placed higher than third.

4. C. Ted Williams. The Splendid Splinter tried his luck on the mound in the first game of a doubleheader against Detroit on August 24, 1940. The second-year Kid did all right, allowing one run in two innings in a 12-1 loss at Fenway. The closest Mike Greenwell got to the mound was as an emergency catcher in his rookie year, 1987.

5. Carl Yastrzemski. Yaz and Brooks Robinson each played 23 years for their respective clubs, with Brooks ending his run in 1977, and Yaz calling it quits in 1983.

6. Manny Ramirez and Carl Yastrzemski. Ramirez hit 41 in 2001, 43 in 2004 and 45 in 2005. Yaz clubbed 44 in 1967, 1969 and 1970. Believe it or not, Jim Rice and Ted Williams each hit 40 homers only once.

7. C. Ted Williams. Teddy Ballgame played 1,984 games in left field for Boston. Other men who have spent the most time in

front of the Green Monster (not counting games at other positions): Yaz (1,913), Jim Rice (1,503) and Mike Greenwell (1,124).

8. Six. It would have been fitting for this number to match Carl Yastrzemski's uniform number, 8, but there were plenty of Presidents in office between 1961 and 1983: John F. Kennedy, Lyndon B. Johnson, Richard M. Nixon, Gerald Ford, Jimmy Carter and Ronald Reagan.

9. John Updike. The Pulitzer Prize-winning author was on hand to document the home run in the last at bat by Ted Williams at the "lyric little bandbox of a ballpark." His fabled story was published in *The New Yorker* a few weeks after Ted's adieu in 1960.

Your Grandfather's Sox

1. B. 1939. The rookie hit .327 and led the majors in RBIs, with 145. By 1941 he was hitting .406.

2. Red Ruffing. He threw six pitches to Ted Williams his first two at bats and struck him out both times. The Kid crushed a Ruffing pitch his third time up for a double that just missed going out of Yankee Stadium on opening day in 1939.

3. A. Howard Ehmke. He went 20-17 for the 1923 Red Sox, who finished a distant eighth in an eight-team league.

4. Pee Wee Reese. Traded to the Brooklyn Dodgers for four players and $35,000 just before his 21st birthday, Reese was the sparkplug on seven pennant winners and finished in the top 10 in the NL MVP voting eight times.

5. A. Cleveland Indians. Bob Lemon was going for his 21st win and had a 12-1 lead at Fenway, but the Red Sox scored eight in the home fourth. With Bob Feller on in the eighth, Walt Dropo's triangle-bound triple tied the game, and Bobby Doerr gave Boston the lead in a 15-14 win. A day earlier, the Tribe had blown a 7-0 lead to the Sox.

6. B. Bill Monbouquette. The day Monbo signed his contract at age 18 in 1955, he was sitting in the stands with his parents when a rude group behind him spilled booze on his mother. He and his father beat up the drunks and were tossed in the Fenway holding tank. Pronouncing his name—and getting the cops to believe him—took some time, but they got it ironed out, and the Medford kid pitched 254 times for the Sox.

7. False. Rogers Hornsby of the Cardinals won the Triple Crown in 1922 and 1925. There was no NL MVP in 1922, but Rajah won it in 1925. Ted lost the MVP to Yankees in both his 1942 and 1947 Triple Crown seasons despite vastly superior numbers.

8. D. .407. A career .344 hitter, he hit under .300 just once (at age 40). He actually surpassed his legendary .406 mark by a point in 1953, though in just 110 plate appearances. He had hit .400 in 12 at bats before going to war in 1951.

9. A. 1941. Ted Williams, who had gone hitless in his first All-Star Game in 1940, doubled in a run early in the '41 game but was caught looking by Claude Passeau in the eighth. He came up in the ninth in Detroit with the AL down a run and two men on with two outs. He hit a Passeau pitch off the third deck and whooped around the bases.

10. C. Tex Hughson. He won 22 games for the 1942 Red Sox and led the team in most pitching categories through 1944 before serving in the military and coming back to win 20 games for the 1946 AL champs.

11. Mel Parnell and Ellis Kinder. After winning 11 of 12, the Sox needed just one win in their last two for the pennant. Parnell (25-7) blew a 4-0 lead and the bullpen took the loss. Kinder (23-6) was down just 1-0 on the last day when New York scored four times in the eighth—especially cruel as the Sox rallied in the ninth but fell short, 5-3.

12. Pumpsie Green. He took the field for Boston for the first time on July 21, 1959, a dozen years after Jackie Robinson's Brooklyn debut. The team passed on numerous African Americans, including Robinson and Willie Mays.

13. D. 1950. The '50 Sox won 94 games and scored more often than any major league club by far, with 1,027 runs, but they finished third behind the Yankees (98 wins) and Tigers (95).

14. True. His temper got him into hot water with fans and the press, but no ump ever thumbed "The Thumper." He was never ejected in four years managing for Washington/Texas.

15. Lou Boudreau. The Indians Hall of Fame player-manager came up with the idea in 1946 of flooding the right side of the infield when Ted Williams came up. Six years later he was hired to manage the Red Sox, while Ted was in Korea.

16. B. Jack Fisher. The Orioles hurler surrendered the eighth-inning home run to Ted Williams, his 521st home run in his 7,706th—and final—at bat. Fat Jack, who'd relieved Steve Barber in the first, took the loss when Boston rallied in the home ninth to give Sox reliever Mike Fornieles the win. Williams had been removed in the top of the ninth.

17. No. He did hit .380 away from Fenway Park, a franchise record. He also hit .428 that year at home. Add it up and you get .406.

18. A. Lee Culberson. He took over in center field after Dom DiMaggio injured his leg during the game-tying rally in the top of the eighth. With the much more agile Dom in there, Enos Slaughter might not have tried to score on the hit off reliever Bob Klinger that cost the Sox the Series.

19. His own mark. Jimmie Foxx knocked in 143 in his first year with Boston in 1936.

20. B. Bill Monbouquette. Monbo's 17 K's in 1961 broke the nine-inning club mark of 15 set by Smoky Joe Wood in 1911. Mickey McDermott fanned 15 in '51, but it was in 16 innings.

Octobers — Great and Tragic

1. B. Ken Holtzman. With Catfish Hunter gone to the Yankees in a bidding war, the A's went with just two starters in the best-of-five ALCS in 1975. The Red Sox pulled away for a 7-1 win against Holtzman in Game 1 in Oakland. Two days later, Holtzman started and lost at Fenway, ending Oakland's championship reign.

2. D. Rick Wise. Boston's Game 3 starter came in the top of the 12th in Game 6 and allowed two hits, but got out of the jam. Carlton Fisk sent everyone home happy a few memorable minutes later.

3. A. Jim Burton. Manager Darrell Johnson's decision to pinch-hit for Jim Willoughby in the eighth and to bring in the rookie lefty, who had pitched to just two batters in October, in the ninth innings of a tie Game 7 will forever be questioned in Red Sox Nation. Joe Morgan's bloop hit off Burton decided the Series.

4. 1918. The Red Sox beat the Cubs in Game 6 of the World Series to clinch their fifth title in 15 years. No world championships have come at home since, but that they finally came

and were both the results of sweeps is all the better for the cardiac health of Red Sox Nation.

5. D. Rudy York. He cracked a three-run home run in the first inning of Game 3 against the Cardinals. The last World Series homer at Fenway Park before that came in Game 7 of the 1912 World Series by New York Giant Larry Doyle—Boston's Larry Gardner hit one earlier that day. (Note: Hank Gowdy homered for the Boston Braves in the 1914 World Series, played at Fenway.)

6. Jim Lonborg. He came within four outs of a no-hitter before Julian Javier broke it up in Game 2 of the 1967 World Series.

7. Babe Ruth. The Babe tossed 14 innings in his World Series debut in Game 2 of the 1916 World Series. The last 13 1/3 innings he did not allow a run. He ran that number to 29 2/3 by 1918, a World Series mark that lasted until Whitey Ford topped it in 1961.

8. B. Harry Hooper. Hoop is the only Red Sox player to play in four World Series: 1912, 1915, 1916, and 1918. He fashioned a 15-game hitting streak over three World Series. Overall, he batted 92 times with 27 hits (.293). Teammate Duffy Lewis had 19 hits in 67 at bats (.283) and holds the team mark with six doubles in World Series play.

9. Pittsburgh Pirates (1903), New York Giants (1912), Philadelphia Phillies (1915), Brooklyn Dodgers (1916), Chicago Cubs (1918), St. Louis Cardinals (2004) and Colorado Rockies (2007). Every Sox fan should have this memorized—and an extra point if you knew Brooklyn's 1915 team was known as the Robins.

Your Great-Grandfather's Sox

1. C. Harvard. The Red Sox topped the Crimson, 2-0, on April 9, 1912, to open Fenway Park, 11 days before the first regular-season game was played there.

2. The Philadelphia Phillies. Pitchers Rube Foster, Dutch Leonard and Ernie Shore went the distance in the five-game victory.

3. Three times. The Babe took the bump for the 1916, 1917 and 1918 openers. The Sox won all three. In 1919 Ruth was the opening day left fielder.

4. D. Tris Speaker. New York Giants catcher Art Wilson dropped the throw that would have nailed Speaker. Instead, Game 2

was tied, only to be called by darkness an inning later. It was replayed from the start and wound up giving Boston five home games in what became an eight-game World Series won by the Sox, 4-3-1.

5. A. Jimmy Collins. A star for the Boston Braves, he jumped to the American League and served as third baseman and manager for most of the club's first six seasons of existence.

6. Six! Starting in 1901, Cy's Sox win totals were 33, 32, 28, 26, 18, 13, 21, 21. That's how a century after retirement his name is still synonymous with pitching excellence—though it helps that the annual trophy rewarding these qualities was named for him.

7. D. 20. The '06 club was the first in franchise history to lose 100 times or finish last. The '07 team was slightly better, losing only 16 straight and 90 games overall.

8. A. Buck Freeman. He led the league with 13 in 1903. Though it sounds modest, that was a higher total than the 10 hit by AL leading Sox sluggers Jake Stahl (1910) and Tris Speaker (1912). Babe Ruth would soon blow them all out of the water.

9. A. 2. That 1917 total was the lowest number of homers Babe Ruth recorded in his 21 full seasons as a player, but manager Ed Barrow made him an everyday player when he wasn't pitching in 1918. Turned out to be a good move.

10. A. Dutch Leonard. His 1914 mark of 0.96 is in fact the lowest over a full season in major league history.

11. C. Smoky Joe Wood. His 1.99 ERA in 1,416 innings is the lowest in franchise history. Cy Young is a very close second, though, with a 2.00 ERA in nearly twice the innings tossed by Smoky Joe.

12. C. Smoky Joe Wood. He was hammered by the Giants in Game 7—there was an extra game because of a tie—but he came on in the eighth in relief of Hugh Bedient and got the win to claim Boston's second championship. Wood allowed a run in the top of the 10th, but Smoky Joe was bailed out by a walkoff win for the ages at Fenway Park.

13. A. Larry Gardner. The slugging Sox third baseman came through after two Giants errors allowed Boston to tie the game in the 10th. Christy Mathewson took the ultimate hard-luck loss, 3-2, in the deciding eighth game.

14. Huntington Avenue Grounds. It was home to the Red Sox from its debut in the new American League in 1901 through the 1911 season, hosting the first modern World Series in 1903.

15. D. Heinie Wagner. Not to be confused with Honus Wagner, Heinie was the regular shortstop for the better part of seven years for the Sox, including the 1912 world champions. In 1916 he joined Bill Carrigan's club as the first full-time coach, though he remained on the roster and played sparingly in 1916 and 1918.

16. Cy Young. They didn't name the award after him for nothing. Bill Dinneen pitched to 1,508 batters in 1902, two more than Cy.

17. C. 29. Babe Ruth shattered the old mark in 1919 and did so with a dead ball and unfriendlier Fenway dimensions than later sluggers would enjoy. Infamously sold to New York, Ruth would club 54 in 1920 as a Yankee.

18. D. 26. And that was in a season shortened to 126 games because of World War I. It also doesn't count being blanked by the Cubs in Game 6 of the World Series. Talk about a dead ball.

19. Eddie Cicotte. A master of the then-legal shine ball, Cicotte went 52-46 with a 2.69 ERA for Boston before being sold to the White Sox in 1912.

20. B. 7. Harry Hooper, who would soon be sent on his way as well, hit 47 fewer home runs in 1920 than his ex-teammate enjoyed at his new digs in New York.

Bonus Section

Boston Golf

1. Which Massachusetts course has hosted the most U.S. Opens?

   A. The Country Club

   B. The International

   C. Myopia Hunt Club

   D. Old Sandwich Golf Club

2. True or false? The first Ryder Cup was held in Worcester.

3. Francis Ouimet became the first American-born player to win the U.S. Open in 1913. And he did it at his hometown course in which town?

   A. Bolton

   B. Brookline

   C. Canton

   D. Worcester

4. What was the name of the Mark Frost book that became a film about U.S. Open champ Francis Ouimet?

A. *A Gentleman's Game*

B. *The Greatest Game Ever Played*

C. *The Legend of Bagger Vance*

D. *Tin Cup*

5. Whose 45-foot putt on the 17th green unleashed a wild celebration by the Americans in the 1999 Ryder Cup "Battle of Brookline"?

A. Jim Furyk

B. Tom Lehman

C. Justin Leonard

D. Tiger Woods

6. What is the only Massachusetts course where the PGA Championship has been held?

A. Blue Hills Country Club

B. The Country Club

C. Myopia Hunt Club

D. Worcester Country Club

7. In 2011, who claimed the first sudden-death play-off winner in the nine-year history of the FedEx Cup-affiliated Deutch Bank Championship at TPC Boston?

A. Chez Reavie

B. Webb Simpson

C. Vijay Singh

D. Tiger Woods

Answers on pages 265-266

Boston Boxing

1. Massachusetts native Rocky Graziano, who retired in 1956 as the undefeated heavyweight champion, was known by what local nickname?

   A. "The Beast from Boston"

   B. "The Marblehead Mauler"

   C. "The Plymouth Rock"

   D. "The Rock from Brockton"

2. This New Bedford-bred fighter recorded a staggering 3,020 punches in a 1993 fight. Who was this light heavyweight punching machine?

   A. "Sucra" Ray Oliveira

   B. Zach Padilla

   C. Vinnie Paz

   D. Willie Pep

3. Which local product remained undisputed middleweight champ from 1980 to 1987?

   A. "Marvelous" Marvin Hagler

   B. Thomas "Hitman" Hearns

   C. Sugar Ray Leonard

   D. Mike Tyson

4. Which Brookline-born middleweight defeated legendary Sugar Ray Robinson twice in six months at Boston Garden in 1960?

   A. Jake LaMotta

   B. Freddie Mack

   C. Floyd Patterson

   D. Paul Pender

5. "The Boston Strong Boy" was the last bare-knuckle fighter, the first to win $1 million in the ring, and supposedly the inspiration for the name "Long Johns" because of the look of his boxing togs. Who was this Boston boxing legend?

6. True or false? The first sporting event at Boston Garden was a boxing match.

7. Which film is based on Lowell boxer Micky Ward?
   A. *The Fighter*
   B. *Raging Bull*
   C. *Requiem for a Heavyweight*
   D. *Rocky*

Answers on pages 266-267

Boston Golf

1. C. Myopia Hunt Club. Founded in 1882, the club had hosted four U.S. Opens before its 30th year—and none since. Located in South Hamilton, Myopia (named for brothers with bad vision) hosted the Open in 1898, 1901, 1905 and 1908. Each of the Opens was won by a Scot.

2. True. Worcester Country Club was the site of the first Ryder Cup in 1927. In the first official match between professionals from America and Great Britain, the U.S. won easily, 9½-2½. Walter Hagen would serve as captain for the first six Ryder Cups.

3. B. Brookline. He grew up across the street from The Country Club and worked there as a caddy. A superb scholastic golfer, his father made him quit school to work in a store. When the club held the 1913 U.S. Open, 20-year-old Ouimet joined the field late, even though he was Massachusetts amateur champion. The kid shocked the world.

4. B. *The Greatest Game Ever Played*. The book—and the movie—is the story of how Francis Ouimet came out of obscurity to defeat two of the greatest pros of the day: Harry Vardon and Ted Ray. Ouimet proved that not only the high-born—or European born—could master the game. And he started golf on a wave of popularity in America.

5. C. Justin Leonard. Leonard's putt halved the match with Europe that led to the narrowest of wins, 14½-13½, in the 1999 Ryder Cup at The Country Club. U.S. captain Tom Lehman is often singled out for leading the charge onto the green at Brookline and the ensuing pandemonium… while the match was still contested.

6. A. Blue Hills Country Club. The Canton course hosted the event in 1956, when the PGA Championship was still a match

play event—and was won by Jack Burke Jr. Two years later the PGA Championship switched to stroke play like most other tournaments.

7. B. Webb Simpson. He earned a playoff when Chez Reavie chunked an approach shot on 18 and then Simpson won in the second hole of the Labor Day playoff. The final is scheduled on Monday, with the four-day tournament starting Friday instead of the usual Thursday-to-Sunday setup.

Boston Boxing

1   D. "The Rock from Brockton." Raised by Italian immigrants in Brockton, Rocky Marciano went on to be the top boxer of his day. He retired with a 49-0 record, 43 wins by knockout, at age 32. He tragically died in a 1969 plane crash the day before he would have turned 47.

2. A. "Sucra" Ray Oliveira. According to CompuBox, he rang up 3,000-plus punches against Zack Padilla in 1993 and set another mark with 1,424 punches of Vince Phillips in 2000. He won both fights at Foxwoods Casino.

3. A. "Marvelous" Marvin Hagler. The southpaw from Brockton went 37 bouts without a defeat following a 1976 loss. Along the way he defeated boxing legends Thomas "Hitman" Hearns, Roberto Duran and John Mugabi, before retiring abruptly in 1987 after losing a controversial split-decision to Sugar Ray Leonard.

4. D. Paul Pender. Hailing from the same town as John F. Kennedy, Pender's greatest moment(s) came months before JFK captured the White House. Pender won split decisions at Boston Garden in January and June of 1960 over the great Sugar Ray Robinson. The only boxer to beat Robinson twice, Pender's career was cut short by brittle hands.

5. John L. Sullivan. Born in Roxbury to Irish immigrants, John Lawrence Sullivan held the heavyweight title from 1881 to 1892, when he lost an epic bout to "Gentleman" Jim Corbett. Sullivan rarely fought without gloves, but he retained his bare-knuckle image because no one after him fought without gloves.

6. True. Boston Garden was built for boxing. Promoter Tex Rickard, who'd built the third incarnation of Madison Square Garden, planned to open venues in several cities. But Rickard died a year after Boston Madison Square Garden was chris-

tened on November 17, 1928, with Dick Finnegan winning the main event over Andre Routis.

7. A. *The Fighter*. The 2010 drama centered on "Irish" Micky Ward (played by Mark Wahlberg) a Golden Gloves fighter who took several years off after a string of defeats. He was trained by his half-brother, Dicky Eklund (Christian Bale) and managed by his mother, Alice Ward (Melissa Leo). It won the Academy Award for Best Supporting Actor (Bale) and Actress (Leo).

How did you do?

THE SECTIONS	YOUR SCORE
THE BRUINS	
Bruins Basics	_____
Fight Night	_____
Your Father's Bruins (worth double)	_____
The Bobby Orr Challenge	_____
Your Grandfather's Bruins (worth double)	_____
The Original Six	_____
THE CELTICS	
Celtics Basics	_____
Your Father's Celtics (worth double)	_____
The Larry Bird Challenge	_____
Your Grandfather's Celtics (worth double)	_____
The Bill Russell Challenge	_____
Celtics in the Rafters	_____
THE COLLEGES	
Boston College	_____
The Holy War	_____
Boston University	_____
Harvard	_____
'The Game'	_____
Northeastern	_____
Beanpot Challenge	_____
College Knowledge	_____

THE PATRIOTS

Patriots Basics _____

The Brady Bunch (of Questions) _____

Your Father's Patriots (worth double) _____

The Super Bowl Challenge _____

Your Grandfather's Patriots (worth double) _____

Pats Firsts _____

THE RED SOX

Red Sox Basics _____

Red Sox by the Numbers _____

Your Father's Sox (worth double) _____

Out of Left Field _____

Your Grandfather's Sox (worth double) _____

Octobers — Great and Tragic _____

Your Great-Grandfather's Sox (worth double) _____

BONUS SECTION

Boston Golf _____

Boston Boxing _____

POINT TOTAL _____

Acknowledgments

You just can't make this stuff up, as they say. In giving as many detailed answers as possible for an array of topics on Boston sports, I used several different resources. Human resources also came in handy, notably Tom Doherty at Cardinal Publishing and my agent Anne Marie O'Farrell at Marcil-O'Farrell for helping put this book in motion. Special thanks to Jeffrey Marcus, who helped me with the Celtics and Greg Spira, who provided assistance with the Red Sox. I'm sad Greg never got to see the finished product, but I know he would have enjoyed it.

Bibliography

Books

Big League Ballparks, Gary Gillete, Eric Enders, et. al (New York: Metro Books, 2009)

Killer B's, Boston Globe 2011 Special Commemorative Book (Chicago: Triumph Books, 2011)

Dynasty's End: Bill Russell and the 1968-69 World Champion Boston Celtics, Thomas J. Whalen (Boston: Northeastern University Press, 2004)

Red Sox by the Numbers, Bill Nowlin et. al, (New York: Skyhorse Publishing, 2010)

Red Sox Threads, Bill Nowlin (Burlington, MA: Rounder Books, 2008)

Total Hockey, Dan Diamond, et. al (Kingston, NY: Total Sports Publishing, 2000)

The Ultimate Red Sox Companion, Gary Gillete and Pete Palmer (eds.), (Hanover, MA: Maple Street Press, 2007)

162-0: The Greatest Wins (Chicago: Triumph Books, 2010)

2011 Red Sox Media Guide
2011 New England Patriots Media Guide
2011-12 Boston College Media Guide

Periodicals

Baseball Digest (though not the "Quick Quiz")
Boston Herald
Maple Street Press Bruins Annual 2011-12
New York Times
Sports Illustrated
Sports Weekly

Websites

baseball-reference.com
basketball-reference.com
beanpothockey.com
boston.com
espn.com
goaliesarchive.com
hockeyfights.com
hockey-reference.com
profootball-reference.com
profootballhof.com
redsoxdiehard.com

And without creating several pages worth of extra urls, let this stand as a thank you to all the web sites for all the colleges in the Boston area.